CW00516146

TABLE OF CONTENTS

6 Quick Power Thoughts To Ponder BEFORE You Complete Your "Million Dollar Day"

10 Stories To Inspire Your Very Own "Million Dollar Day"

6 More Products And Experiences From The Hoverson Brand

6 Quick Power Thoughts to Ponder
BEFORE You Complete Your "Million Dollar Day"

Power-Thought #1:

"If you made a comprehensive list of EVERYTHING you've been procrastinating on...and were told you'd be given ONE MILLION dollars if you completed the entire list in a 24-hour period...could you do it?"

When I was a child, my parents would have me do a myriad of chores around the farm. Before I was allowed to go to baseball practice, I would have to mow and weed-whack our 4-acre lawn.

Before I could leave the house to play with friends, the kitchen had to be cleaned perfectly (no dishes in the sink or the dishwasher, all the counters wiped off, the floors swept, etc.). It was the 1980's, but my parents still had old-school ideas about the capacity and importance of kids working.

Before I could go to my friends, I had to weed the garden and clean out two horse stalls. During the North Dakota winters, the dung would freeze rock solid. I'd only clean those about once a month, so the dung would reach about one-foot high and cover nearly all of the 10ft by 10ft stalls.

In order to penetrate this frozen fecal fortress, I would take a spear-like iron rod about 5 feet long (not sure where we obtained it), and hurl it like a javelin into the icy dung. Usually, after only a few throws, I'd create a crack in the ice-dung-block, and then begin chiseling away to clear every ounce of manure away until a perfectly cleaned wooden floor was the only thing you could see.

Like many kids, I hated chores. However, I also hated feeling that feeling. Thus, *I began to imagine that I had a world-class business, and that I was paid one million dollars each time I completed a task because it was done so beautifully*.

This imaginary game lifted my mindset. It motivated me. It felt real. I pretended film crews were videoing me while I worked and that the whole world was watching. I imagined announcers (just like sports announcers) were enthusiastically commenting moment by moment as I exerted a swift and fierce effort into my task. It gave me pride in my work. It converted my attitude from "eh" to "excited."

Admittedly, the whole idea of a 10-year-old kid thinking like this is as bombastic as it is ridiculous.

However, once I imagined a gigantic incentive (like being paid a million dollars and being admired for my work) my energy activated.

Prior to the invention of the game, the chores felt dreary and heavy. Once I began playing this "million dollar" game (starting around age 10), my focus sharpened. I'd listen to the Beatles "Greatest Hits" in my Sony Walkman and work like a hurricane.

Fast-forward from childhood to the current day. By age 37, I've created 6 distinct products and brands that have all earned over $1,000,000 each. My educational "how-to" videos have been viewed over 1,000,000 hours.

Is it possible that simply "pretending" to be paid one million dollars can lift your energy? Can it possibly even set the stage for you to earn millions, not in your mind, but in real-life? We will get back to this idea in the pages ahead.

Power-Thought #2:

In high school, I remember reading a Thomas Edison quote that sparked a fire inside me to experiment with human potential. The quote was simple:

"If you did everything you were capable of doing, you'd literally astonish yourself."

Edison's creative marathon earned him 1093 patents over his lifetime. He was the first human voice to be recorded by a machine (he said, "Mary had a little lamb."). So if you like listening to recordings of music, you can thank Edison.

He also invented movies. Literally.

The term "movies" is derived from "moving pictures" because prior to movies, we only had pictures. But Edison's pictures could move… which astonished people. If you like movies, Edison is the pioneering patriarch to that technology.

But let's get back to his quote, "If you did everything you were capable of doing, you'd literally astonish yourself."

One of the most common choruses that arise after someone completes their "Million Dollar Day" (MDD) is some version of, "I had no idea I could get so much done in a 24-hour period."

The MDD is designed to create astonishment in yourself, and possibly astonishment from others as they marvel at the breadth, depth and volume of your creative output.

Power-Thought #3:

"The Million Dollar Day Makes Meditation Easier"

Meditation takes many forms and has many methodologies. One of the most descriptive illustrations of meditation is the idea that our daily life is like the surface of the ocean: windy, choppy, loud, a little chaotic, unpredictable and noisy.

But, when we meditate, we slowly allow our minds and bodies to still the chaotic stresses of the here and now as we sink into the quiet and peaceful heart of the ocean depths, where we can access the vast resources that exist inside our spirit. It is in this zone where many of us are able to "Be still, and know that I am God..." (Ps. 46:10).

Once we reach this profound state of calm, the stress melts. In this meditative state, the neurons of our mind begin to light up like a Christmas tree as our mind begins to weave new answers to questions we have.

In this state, strength is restored into us before we ascend back to the surface of our daily life with renewed energy and clarity to live more fully and freely.

It sounds beautiful in theory, and it's even more beautiful in practice. But the deeper levels of chaos and baggage we have on the surface of our lives, the harder and harder it is to escape it and relax ourselves into a state of peace and stillness.

The more chaotic and cluttered our lives are, the more out of control we feel. Consequently, the more we yearn for the type of peace and tranquility meditation can bring us.

The effects of prolonged procrastination contribute to the chaos as the list of "undone", "unfinished", and "unstarted" projects continue to pile on top of each other until it can feel utterly hopeless that we will ever complete them all, let alone keep up with daily tasks that face us every morning.

So when it comes to meditation, the chaos we have on the surface begins to act like a fleet of buoys that tether our minds to the scattered "surface" reality of our lives. Which makes it REALLY HARD to sink into the deep and glorious meditative state.

But after you complete your first Million Dollar Day, you will feel a massive reset on the "surface." The daily chaos will be replaced with manifested order all around you: your bedroom, your kitchen, your finances, your garage, your car, your businesses, your relationships and more.

In this new state, the surface is peaceful (not only in a physiological or spiritual way, but in tangible reality as your physical and digital environments sparkle with order).

After just one fully engaged Million Dollar Day, your comprehensive habitat will create and give you a platform peace. Your surroundings will have a meditative aura as they are clutter and chaos-free.

If you have a meditative practice, you will discover that after your first Million Dollar Day, you will be able to glide into a meditative state easier and faster than you ever imagined. The Million Dollar Day appears to be about "outer peace", but it ends up becoming a gateway to "inner peace."

Power-Thought #4

"The Seventy Thousand Pound Strawberry"

The average strawberry weighs about .05 pounds (which means it takes about 20 strawberries to equal a pound). In other words, they are pretty light.

Now imagine your assignment was simply to pick up the strawberry, fully extend your hand out in front of your face for 3 seconds, and then bring the strawberry into your mouth and eat it.

The total time the task takes is about 3-10 seconds (an extra few seconds are added to select your strawberry, chew and swallow it). The effort the task requires is minimal. In fact, it feels more like a pleasure than a task.

But now, instead of holding it out in front of you for 3 seconds, you hold out, extended in front of your face for 3 minutes. Suddenly, the strawberry feels a little bit heavier. But, it's a doable task. No biggie. But not as easy as the 3-second version.

Now, let's say you hold it out in front of your face for 3 hours. Very quickly, the task becomes burdensome as your hand and arms tighten, and your face begins to sweat.

Okay, let's go with holding it out in front of your face for 3 weeks. The task now becomes unbearable.

Extend it to 3 years, and the little task now feels like a daunting giant. It's difficult. It's painful. It's impossible.

Procrastination works in a similar way. Let me explain:

Most of the stuff we want to do in our lives is pretty easy.

Take something like completing your legal will. At it's most basic level (depending on the state and laws of the land), you can;

#1- just Google a template of a basic will to complete (1-min).

#2- Go through line by line and fill in the details of your wishes for your property and items (let's say each item takes 2-10 minutes each).

#3- go to the post office and have it notarized (with drive time and waiting in line...maybe 30-minutes).

#4- You are done. It's a pretty easy process to have "something" in place compared to "nothing" at all. Remember, you can always improve upon it and add to it later. The whole experience will probably lead you to spend 10-min and a few bucks to have a lawyer put some added legal fairy dust on it (but you can do that later).

Yet, the longer and more we "think" about the task, the bigger and heavier it becomes. We stall and delay (we have T.V. shows to watch or something).

The next thing you know, 10 years goes by and you still have no will even though you decided a long time ago you should write up a will.

My Grandpa once told me, "Mark, thinking about doing something is miserable. Actually doing it isn't that big of a deal. And the beer tastes better at night when you are done with it."

Procrastination has a way of making .05 ounce strawberries weigh 70,000 pounds.

Let me press this idea a bit further.

When Shanny and I got married, I surprised her with an original love song during the ceremony (I wrote her the day before the wedding). It's a simple acoustic guitar song with a few verses.

About 5 years ago, I had an idea to hop into a professional recording studio and record it (with a few members of the philharmonic next to me to spice it up a bit). Once this was recorded, I would surprise her with a professionally done fantasy song that she could enjoy forever.

But, I let the idea sit. It's been in the back of my mind for 5 years (approximately 1825 days).

During this period, the idea didn't change, but for some reason, it began to feel very complex, very expensive, very difficult, and almost reached a place of an "impossible idea."

So, this morning (literally a few hours ago), I called a nearby professional studio and shared my idea to take over the studio for about 3 hours to come up with a finished product). The call took 5-minutes and the price was laughably low.

I then reached out to a philharmonic director. Within 10-minutes, he referred me to a better studio designed for orchestra instruments. He then referred me to a guy who he felt could create an accompaniment for a quartet to go along with my song.

Following that phone call, I called the accompaniment guy and explained the vision (10-minute phone call) and he's in love with the idea.

As I type this now, I told him I'd send him a raw and unprofessional version of the song within 48 hours. He's eager to get in on this idea, and said he'd respond in 1 or 2 days max with his ideas.

The entire process, including me practicing up my skills and prepping my voice, along with the 3 hours in the recording studio, and the whole shebang will be less than 10-15 hours of creative spend.

The project is looking way cheaper than I intended. And is actually much more interesting than I originally thought.

I allowed a very simple idea I had 5 years ago to morph into a monster that kept getting punted down the field of time...when all that was required to give oxygen to the idea was a 10-minute phone call.

On your MDD, you may not fully "finish" every task and idea you've ever had, but you will be able to open and energize every idea you've ever had. Whether it's getting a basic will, or writing a dream song for your spouse.

Like eating the strawberry, almost every task we think of is fairly easy, especially when it's broken down into steps. But the longer we don't take tangible action on any idea, the heavier and more complex it begins to feel...until it is suffocated and buried in the "someday" file.

The redeeming factor is when we begin to complete these tasks, the feelings of peace and power and hope and creativity literally explode inside us.

The MDD often awakens a dormant, action-orientated superhero, that is waiting to rise inside you. The residual effects of the day often begin a "domino-effect" that alters the rest of our lives.

Power-Thought #5

"Great Time vs. Common Time"

In ancient religious teaching, there is an idea of "secular" things (which are common things, typically of no everlasting value or spiritual use), and there are "sacred" things (which have long-lasting value and are of spiritual importance).

Without going too deep into the division of that which is "secular" vs. "sacred", we will transition into the idea that not all TIME is created equal. It falls into "great time" compared to "common time."

Let me explain:

The 10-hours of creative spend I invest in reproducing our wedding song in a professional studio with philharmonic musicians yields a piece of "work" that will endure in our family for at least a couple generations (my wife and at least a couple of my kids will find it a sacred keepsake).

Those 10 hours would be considered "Great Time" because the production of that time yields to a potentially long-lasting important unit of work. It also contributes to the bigger narrative of love and legacy and marriage.

10 hours spent staring at what other people are doing on social media doesn't require the same amount of creative spend that producing the song does, but it also tends to lead to very little lasting value. This would be classified as "Common Time" ←this time is okay and unavoidable because we are intellectually unable to live in "Great Time" all the time because it tends to deplete the glucose our brains require to function.

10 Hours watching television are again okay, and it's possible that they contribute to "Great Time" later if a show inspires to you create new initiatives in your life.

For instance, I enjoy the legendary television series "Game of Thrones." I watch all the episodes with interest and even fascination.

Because of Game of Thrones, which weaves long stories of family legacies as they strive to put heirs on the ultimate Iron Throne…because of that show, it got me thinking deeper about legacy.

Here's the short story:

An Eagle Scout recently constructed a quaint gazebo on the property of a beautiful church in my hometown in North Dakota. The same church we were married in and several generations of my family attended.

I have 4 children, and I thought it would be a lovely addition to plant 4 oak trees to surround the gazebo. And space them just far enough away from each other that eventually they would merge their branches together to create a sort of covering over the gazebo.

The idea is that once they are planted (purchasing young trees about 15 feet tall), I would bring our children there and share that our ancestors helped build this town and this church. Then, I would share a few pieces of Scripture about how we are called to become Oak Trees in the world.

In my mind, the conversation would end with a proposed idea that once per year (or so) we would return to this special space and have a conversation about the family legacy.

So what happened?
I took immediate action on my idea, and when I talked with the pastor and landscaping guy at the church, the idea got a soft "nod", but I could tell it would have to go through a couple church board meetings, and the landscaping guy viewed it as adding work to his job.

So, I let the idea simmer. And then I was driving by the highway and spotted a mound of gigantic stone boulders (just a little bit smaller than a small 2-door vehicle).

I got the pricing on purchasing 4 of those boulders, and transporting them into an 11-acre forest our family owns next to a river.

And now, we are going to get 4 boulders to be curiously spaced out, next to literally dozens of 100+ year old oak trees, situated by a river.

This solution, although different from my first idea, is easier, and about the same price. And the boulders will last thousands of years compared to the oak trees which will only last a couple hundred years tops.

The point? Spending a couple hours researching the price of oak trees, boulders, transportation, talking with the church, and finding an alternative…all took less than 2 hours of Great Time.

The results? A neat story that my children will have to physically show and share with their children. It is a sacred thing to me, and to them as well.

View your Million Dollar Day as "Great Time". Use it as an opportunity to launch "Great Time" ideas…one's that last possibly for generations.

Power-Thought #6

"Neuroplasticity & the MDD"

In the year 2010, we built a home in a quiet, newly formed community outside of Phoenix, AZ.

We were the 8th home built in a master-planned community that was slated to have over 1200 homes in it.

When we first arrived, it was stunningly quiet. We bought the kids a motorcycle, and they would ride about one minute down the sidewalk and have hundreds of acres of vast desert wilderness to scoot around in. We would buy clay pigeons and launch them in the air and shoot them with our guns in this wild and free area.

But very shortly, the economy began to recover and there was a super-nova of new homes. Dozens and dozens being built simultaneously. Suddenly, the quiet desert was filled with machines making roads and preparations for the expansion of the community. Our desert play-ground disappeared almost overnight.

All this was well and fine. However, one day, while exiting our neigh-borhood, I noticed a line of cars about half a mile long waiting to turn "left" onto the only exit road from the community.

There was no stop light in place, and it was a two lane road. The con-gestion of traffic seemed almost unbearable.

Then, we left for the summer.

[Every summer, the Hoverson tribe exiles ourselves from the oven-heat of Arizona, and flees to our roots in the Dakotas. We spend a few months there gardening, having bonfires, golfing, drinking, canoeing, fishing, painting, and sort of chilling out.]

When we returned back to AZ a few months later, we noticed the old two lane road became a 6 lane road, and a flurry of new traffic lights were in place.

Immediately, even through there was now even more homes, and more cars, and more people…there was zero congestion, zero traffic issues, and everything was calmer and more beautiful.

So, how does this relate to neuroplasticity & the MDD?

Neuroplasticity, in short, is a term that describes the capacity of the brain create new neural pathways to adapt to new realities.

In other words, our brains have current pathways (similar to roads). All the information in our lives travels on these electric roads. These are basically the existing infrastructure for how we interpret and deal with our lives.

However, the idea of neuroplasticity, is that our brains are somewhat "plastic" (aka- stretchy and able to form new electrical roads).

Very similar to how the two-lane road in our community created a clogged and traffic-jammed reality, so does our mind (with our current road system) can feel completely overwhelmed with "things to do", so much so that we may feel we live in a clogged and jammed reality. In such a state, the goal becomes just to survive the day and not fall further behind on the dreams of our hectic lives.

But the MDD, once we engage it, can create a flurry of new roads and systems in the infrastructure of our mind.

Thus, although it may feel impossible to wipe out all the procrastination that is clogged up in our life, once we attack our procrastination list with a vengeance, we can emerge with not only "cleared" roads, but even new roads, capable of MUCH more abundance in every area of our life.

If you would have told me years ago, that I would have multiple brands that all created over one million dollars AND that my physical presence is rarely required to make any of the brands operate on a daily basis, I would say it was an impossible dream.

However, as I began to purge the past and the undone, I found a new capacity rise within me, capable of achieving more impact and wealth than I ever imaged.

Thousands of our people who have completed a Million Dollar Day report similar results. New ideas sprang forward. New time seemed to open up. With the anchors of past lifted, the future becomes more brilliant.

This is a common sensation upon the completion of your first MDD, and I'm excited to hear about your results too.
So, how EXACTLY do you complete your first Million Dollar Day?

We have a 90-minute video course that guides you through the how and why much more fully than I am able to inside this short book, but I want to give you simple way to get a crack on it.

The video course takes you through several areas of your life, one at a time, and prods you with examples of common "procrastination" areas featuring each area.

In this chapter, I will give you the short version, it's complete enough for you to begin right away (although I do recommend you invest in the $37 course because it adds a marvelous dimension to the barebones written approach below, but here we go).

http://milliondollardaybook.com/

Here are the 7 key areas we address while forming our MDD list:

#1- Basic Health
#1a-Advanced Health

#2- Basic Living Area
#2a- Advanced Living Area

#3- Basic Existing Business
#3a- Advanced New Business

#4- Money

#5- Technology

#6- Relationships

#7- Hobbies, Passions, and Adventures

#8- Miscellaneous Odds & Ends

Below we will charge through each area with a small sample of idea-joggers (primarily sourced from previous MDD participants). Feel free to write on this book and use it as a vehicle to begin building your pro-crastination breakthrough list right now.

Basic Health

Some common items:

*Schedule chiropractor visit for aching lower back
*Schedule massage for knots in my neck
*Schedule dentist for cleaning and Xrays
*Contact Dr. for sleep apnea issues
*See Dr. for hearing issues
*See optometrist for eye-checkup
*Annual physical
*Get health insurance plan
*Price-shop new health insurance plan
*Get complete blood work test
*Check moles

*Freeze off warts

Advanced Health/Body

*Get professional teeth-whitening at Dentist
*Start taking probiotics
*Start taking nutritional supplements
*Try a week of home-delivered healthy meals
*Do reflexology treatment, purchase foot massager
*Get manicure and pedicure
*Try new shampoo
*Try new skin care system
*Hire one month with a personal trainer
*Use gym membership 2 times per week
*Experiment with sensory-deprivation chamber session
*Calculate Body Mass Index, Body Fat Percentage, etc.
*Get consultaion for "Mommy Tuck", Hair Transplant, Hair Removal, Electrolysis, Breast Implants, All things plastic surgery, do a Brazilian wax, whatever ;)

Basic Living Area (Household Property)

*It's best to physically walk through each room and spot EVERY-THING that you are dissatisfied with instead of attempting this from memory
*Clean out junk drawer
*Deep clean fridge and behind fridge
*Deep clean Garage
*Deep clean Car (all junk out of trunk, dashboards, under seats, literally show-room ready standard (Hint: you may feel like you have a new car afterward)
*Empty closet of EVERY clothing item that doesn't make me feel sexy and fresh (donate rest to Goodwill or have a garage sale)
*Change light bulbs so EVERY bulb in the house is active
*Remove annoying stuff in the yard that is broken or in disrepair (either fix or throw away). Examples: birdfeeders, water fountains, flour pots with no flowers in them, anything that is an eye-sore
*Throw away EVERY unused item in the bathroom (outdated skin care bottles, old gross brushes, broken curling irons, etc)
*Sell or donate unused home gym gadgets we never use that are stacked with clothes and eye-sores

*Shampoo all carpets
*Repaint spot on wall that's been bugging me
*Hang that painting we have sitting in the garage
*Fix door handle that's broken and door that won't close properly
(Mark's Hint: every few months, we scan the entire house and make an exhaustive list of EVERYTHING not up to par in the house, and just have a handyman deal with it).
*Replace old air filters, vacuum cleaner filters

Advanced Living Area (Household Property)

*Donate old furniture and finally buy my dream reading chair, dream table, dream chandelier, dream microwave, dream washer-dryer
*Put in new window in the bathroom for better ventilation
*Add a new rug to living room to spruce it up
*Find Grandma's old painting and hang it in the living room
*purchase a year's worth of fire-wood for bonfires
*Tune piano
*Purge all old books I don't read or like anymore
*Get a new bookshelf
*Buy some new crystals to place by our bedside, study, etc
*Through away all old cleaning products and go 100% green with cleaning products
*Buy a new fish tank for our entryway
*Purchase $200 of new plants to improve air quality in house
*Cut down old ugly bushes and put in some fruit trees
*Start new micro-garden on our balcony
*Purchase some new posters for entertainment room
*Frame Degree and Hang in Hallway
*Take old kids shirts and make a fun blanket out of them for a keep-sake (any little creative legacy-like project like that)
*Purchase essential oil infuser and oils for night-time and morning
*Get new bed, or at least comfy new sheets, towels, pillows

Basic Existing Business

*Read new book how to use the tax advantages of a home business & get free consultation with new tax strategist
*Form an LLC, or S-corp
*Get disability insurance

*Apply for business credit card
*Start separate business checking account that is 100% separate from personal accounts
*Get ink and paper for printer. Get new printer.
*Get new app so I can send faxes through my phone
*Close old bank account for past business
*Call IRS to get on payment plan for taxes
*Clean old computer or get new one that is fast
*Terminate expensive employee
*Get a new email and start from scratch, or totally clean old emails out
*Send personal gratitude messages to my existing client base
*Have my past 3 tax returns re-examined by a new accountant for free to see if there was stuff we missed
*Put all my passwords in one place
*Start a skeleton of a succession plan in case of my death

Advanced Business

*Place first ad campaign on Facebook
*Make branding video for our main product
*Schedule to attend industry-leading live event
*Purchase that business course or class I've been wanting
*Schedule out promotion schedule for the next 6 months
*Collect on unpaid invoices
*Cancel outside obligations I don't enjoy that eat time
*Hire a business growth coach or join local mastermind
*Start skeleton of new book to write: Title and Chapters
Money
*Calculate true networth
*Beef up retirement plan
*Boost life insurance for total peace of mind
*Sell high-value items that are not in use (boat, motorcycle, jewelry, watches, etc)
*Do a full audit of all our expenses
*Prepare budget
*Take wealthy/trusted/smart friend out to lunch to ask about what to do with your money
*Cut fat on any unused services
*Refinance Home
*Sell Home
*Meet with potential investor

*Prepare a detailed legal will
*Purchase stock in company you've been eyeing
*Attempt to take your knowledge and turn it into an info-product (almost every area of expertise has a market for information products)
*Attempt to put your business online
*Have a garage sale
*Fully clean out my wallet/purse (or get a new one)

Technology

*Completely "audit" my phone (delete old pictures and transfer pictures to harddrive, delete old apps, update new apps, take contacts out of my phone I'll never reach out to again, fix cracked screen, see if I can get a better service plan)
*Debug my computer 100% so it runs faster
*Get a new computer
*Clear out voicemails
*Create new voicemail and screensaver
*Delete old files from computer
*Transfer VHS tapes into DVD form for posterity
*Get new apps (guitar tuner, food tracker, running apps)
*Backup all computer into a harddrive
*Get all my stuff connected to the cloud
*Attend a free class at an Apple store to learn how to better use my ipad, iphone, photoshop, etc
*Call cable guy to come and make the cable work faster
*Price out my dream computer
*Purge my Facebook friends that annoy me
*Throw away all old cords, chargers, phone cases, old phones, old computers, gadgets that just clog up space
*Get new car charger, on-the-go-chargers, etc
*Get new wireless headset for phone calls

Relationships

*Ask yourself: who is waiting on me for something right now? Make a list and fulfil the promise/obligation
*Ask yourself: who am I waiting on for something right now? Make a list and do a full-court-press on why you require it done now

*Ask yourself: what friend do I owe any money too that I am behind on? Reach out to them and make a small earnest payment stating you intend to get current with them (Or, ask if you can barter with some other form of value...like perform a service that equates to the dollar amount that they are satisfied with)

*Ask yourself, who have I hurt? Is it possible and wise to reconnect with a meaningful apology and some form of "make-up" gift or act? (For instance, an old friend and you fell out of fellowship but you send him/her a letter and take responsibility for your end and then give them a $30 gift certificate to their favorite restaurant or something.

*Who have felt like thanking for their influence in your life. Write them a quick letter with a little gift or momento of your appreciation (the Hoverson's do this all the time and it adds to the magic of life).

*Do you have an aunt, or cousin, or brother, or parent that you've fallen out of sorts with because of someone else? For instance, one MDD person said she grew up loving her auntie, but her aunt and Mom had a falling out when she was in high school, so on her MDD she reconnected with her aunt to say how much she loved her and whatever happened between her Mom and her aunt has no bearing on how much she values and loves her aunt.

*What is a hard/loving "intervention" you've been meaning to have with a friend/family member, but you haven't taken the courage to have the talk yet? Approach it humbly...

Hobbies, Passions, Adventures

*What is a childhood activity you LOVED, and have thought about rekindling, but life has gotten in the way? Example: canoeing, camping, hiking, painting, playing an instrument, drawing, gardening, birding, scouting

*What is some gear that you could purchase, or dust-off and clean to rekindle your passions? Example: pull out the paint brushes and paints and canvas and soon enough...you will find yourself painting. Air up the tires on the old bike, fill up the air in the football, put a new net on the basketball hoop, get a new set of darts, all of this primes the pump for more fun

*Where have you dreamt of traveling? Price out plane tickets and accommodations and you may discover it's much more affordable than you thought.

*What are some old books that lit a fire in your heart at one point, dig them out and set them around the house again (in the bathroom, in the living room, in the kitchen, in the study, you may find your old passions reignited).
*What are local adventures that others travel to your area to experience but you still haven't done them? Become a localvore (someone who doesn't have their eyes only on the ends of the earth, but engages in the richness of their locality).

Miscellaneous

Open your mind to literally EVERYTHING you've wanted to do, or thought to do, or have been procrastinating on.

Everything.

Don't be scared of your list.

Your old system of thinking (based on the old infrastructure of your mind) will feel the list is IMPOSSIBLE, and it will want to shriek away from even making the list.

But remember neuroplasticity, your mind has a unique capacity to build new, massively regenerated and modernized infrastructure, that can wipe out your entire list.

Your first Million Dollar Day usually reveals an ocean of more items you haven't thought of. Very soon though, you will find yourself almost entirely occupied in the fabulous "here and now" with a heart bursting with hope for the future.

10 Stories To Inspire Your
Very Own "Million Dollar Day"

Amparo Titmus

When Amparo shared her MDD story with me, I was gripped by her very interesting story of meeting Paul McCartney and her collection of Beatles memorabilia. She has a beautiful spirit and it oozes through the next few pages.

Her story shares many interesting details of how her MDD changed her life. But two things stick out to me more than all others:

#1- Her vast and curious trove of Beatles memorabilia was literally packed away. It was inactive. No one was enjoying it. But on her MDD, when she rediscovered her treasury of Beatles lore, she gave it to her sister. Her sister's husband is a serious musician. With the gift from Amparo, he was able to deck his studio out with original Beatles relics. Now, he is able to record his music surrounded with the near-magical relics of music history. Not only does it give him an extra shot of inspiration, when guests see his studio, it automatically pops with extra mystique. Bottomline: her MDD recaptured, restored, and reactivated thousands of dollars of treasure. This type of story echoes through many MDD tales.

#2- In her 10 Tips, she emphasizes recruiting help (paid or bartered) to help expedite the list. This tip is revolutionary for many of us who are accustomed to doing everything "by ourselves." When you make speed one of the highest values in your life, your mind will marvel you with it's ability to produce creative solutions. Recruiting help will make your MDD blast forward.

Amparo's warm and caring spirit covers the next few pages.

Our home had been our sanctuary. It represented not only the place where we raised our three young children but an extended family home. The thought of losing the home that I loved, the home my children loved, the heart of my family was devastating to me but I prepared to let go and began purging my material possessions and distributing the family treasures. That is just one of the things I did on my Floridian Million Dollar Day. When the last of 8 trips to the Goodwill was done, the garage sale signs were gone and my daughter and sisters had driven away with all my family photos, collectibles, books and many beloved possessions, yep even my Beatles collection, my Paul McCartney autographs, I sat with my record book and began my next plan of action: create a budget with the "new found money" I would now have that I had chosen not to pay my mortgage. As I visualized the ins and outs of my finances my stomach churned and burned but my mind was racing and what happened afterwards was unexpected.

With my children grown and gone, my house had become a place filled with "stuff" yet it felt empty. My intention on my Million Dollar Day was to clear out all the items that had accumulated over the last 25 years. I had been working away from home for years and the house and surrounding property needed much maintenance.

In 1990, I graduated nursing school and enabled us to purchase our dream home in the woods of Central Florida. A place where we could raise our three young children away from the risks of city life, to appreciate nature, enjoy the peace and comforts of the Earth. The reality that we would be able to have our children live in a home with a large pool and huge oak trees in our own acre of land was beyond anything I had ever been able to imagine.

I began working away from home to make even more money on assignments 4–6 hours away, 3–4 days a week. Within a few years, after our divorce, I started traveling cross country so that I could continue to pay the mortgage and keep our family home. I had accumulated $95,000 of credit card debt. The extra income had given me a false sense of security regarding money and I had started traveling overseas, enjoying the pleasures of meeting new people and meeting one of my childhood idols, Paul McCartney, several times I might add, and began a serious collection of Beatles memorabilia.

Having grown up in the South Bronx, money did not interest me. It was just something I never thought I would have so I never learned how to manage it. So I spent it.

I missed a lot of good times, times with my family.

Our home had always been occupied by at least one of my children and one or more of their friends. This only made me more determined to keep Casa Madre, the name my kids gave it.
No matter how much time had passed or how far anyone had traveled, it was the one place we could all come "home" to. My biggest goal was to pay off my debt and move back home. After all, I had managed before, why couldn't I do it again? Besides that, something odd had begun to happen. I was no longer happy being a nurse.

In my nursing career I had pretty much done it all but the joy was gone. I dreaded going to work. I would actually have physical ailments, headaches, nausea, general malaise. I realized I resented my job, resented being away from home, resented abiding by rules and practices that were liability driven and not patient driven. In a nutshell, I was miserable and was rapidly beginning to hate what I once loved so much. I began to look for ways to generate an income and possibly change careers.

In January of 2014 I began to study the teachings of Mark Hoverson. Now let's be real here, I didn't read or watch a course and everything changed for me overnight. But a gradual process began as I gradually began to comprehend what was being shared. It had even greater impact when I began to actually do what I was being told to do. Funny how that is, isn't it?

The Million Dollar Day is one of the early lessons in Mark's teachings and I believe I watched it at least 8 or 10 times before I actually fully comprehended the significance of the activities.

Amparo Titmus's Results

My first Million Dollar Day brought me home. I had been in California for nearly 4 years, traveling a total of 12 years. I came home only to find that everything had changed. It no longer made sense to keep the house.

Just last year I had paid off the last of my credit card debt and the balance of my truck I was debt free except for the mortgage and student loans. I couldn't help but ask myself the burning questions. What had changed? How could it be that I could no longer afford my mortgage payments especially now when my son and his young pregnant wife were now seeking refuge at Casa Madre? It wasn't easy, but as I sat with my record book, the answers were undeniably staring at me

Today, just 4 months later, I am caught up with the mortgage. My son and his wife lives in my home with their two boys, Luke is just over 2 months old. They will be moving on to their home soon and I will be listing the house as a rental property for another family to create their memories. I am grateful that I have been able to provide this sanctuary for my children and my grandchildren. My son actually told me yesterday how surreal it is to do things with his children in the home he remembers doing them with his siblings.

As for me? I am just beginning to enjoy life.

Amparo Titmus' 10 Tips

#1- Always begin at the beginning. Watch the Million Dollar Day video repeatedly, as many times as necessary and when you think you get it, watch it again.

#2- Make your list as specific as possible. Your list should be as detailed as possible in all the areas that are required in the instructions. List the outcome desired and how it will be accomplished.

#3- Make as many preparations beforehand. Make arrangements for anything that could become an obstacle or an interruption such as arranging for childcare, gather necessary supplies such as storage bins, trash bags. With your personal care items, make the appointments and show up.

#4- Start early and concentrate on each task on your list individually before you move on to the next. Remain focused and cross them off your list as they are completed. Actually seeing that you are making progress will make you feel accomplished and motivated you to keep going.

#5- Recruit help. Know that you can hire and delegate others to help you in exchange for either monetary compensation or something as simple as a meal. My brother-in-law replaced the support beams of my back porch in exchange for dinner and a swim, after I resuscitated it from pond state.

#6- Don't ignore those things you first think of. These are the things that tend to weigh heaviest on our minds.
#7- Address the personal items. Taking care of oneself is the most important thing we can do and all too often it is the thing we tend to procrastinate on the most.

#8- Blast some music that will energize you.

#9- Plan to eat healthy meals, drink lots of water throughout the day.

#10- Get adequate rest the night before. Read a good book and be at peace.

About Amparo Titmus

Amparo Pagan Titmus RN MSN/ed is an entrepreneur, a nurse leader and educator. She is the founder of Global Healing Hands and has dedicated herself to creating a holistic sanctuary for women. It will be called Casa Madre.

Website: AmparoTitmus.com

Christine Kominiak

Christine's MDD story is so full of unexpected twists, candor, and a little dose of hilarity. If I was forced to select two pieces of her experience that gripped me most, they are:

#1- Her risky, but honest, telling of her underwear scenario. In marketing, we've learned that if you place slices of apples in clear plastic bags and also placed them in colorful and stylish plastic bags, nearly 100% of people select the slices of apples from the decorative packaging. Christine, in great detail, shares how her old panties were basically inadequate packaging. And upon reviving her panty portfolio, not only did she feel sexier, her husband Matthew also appreciated the effort. Which led to a bit of a renaissance in their romantic life. Hint to guys and girls: better packaging makes whatever is packaged automatically more appealing. ;)

#2- Christine's raw candor about the fact that she was a highly-paid "productivity" expert to top brands and companies, but when she engaged the MDD philosophy, she was shocked. Most productivity stuff is band-aid-like help at best. The MDD is deliberately designed to be a day of soul-shaking, mind-altering, life-resetting results. It is like a nuclear bomb on procrastination vs. a nice "bit-by-bit" approach which fails to reset the nervous system or awaken new physic energy for creating an newer and brighter future.

Tons of value packed in these next few pages.

Not many years ago I trained productivity and organization skill sets and mindsets to Fortune 1000 companies, a government agency that required background checks for security clearance, and a state university, and other small to large businesses. I was hired by these high-efficiency organizations and received consistent feedback of gratitude from their staff, expressing that they were no longer dropping important things through the cracks, and that they were able to find anything in their offices within seconds because of the work we did together. You can say that I was in the center of a high-level productivity world. And it was because of this that I believed that not only could I teach it, but that my own life was a well-oiled, productivity machine, free of clutter and available for loads of opportunity.

But none of that mattered now, as a wife working online from home. I felt I might as well have never learned a thing about focus, organization and productivity because I couldn't make a single decision without becoming exhausted. And of the decisions that were made, only came after days, weeks and months of putting them off, adding to more mental overload and stress. I wanted to be a fast action-taker and completer, who wouldn't want this? But at this time in my life I couldn't be further from that dream.

Then, I was introduced to "The Famous Million Dollar Day." I didn't expect to learn anything new when it came to physical organization, but it's funny that the physical stuff is what helped me see obstacles in other aspects of my life, including my business and relationships. Initially I thought this was "just another productivity or de-cluttering course," but in less than 24 hours, my mental framework was rocked and disrupted my deep-rooted beliefs about productivity.

It's laughable to know that I used to teach, and consult with people on productivity (and get paid well for it), and to have never "got" what came from my Million Dollar Day. My soul was given permission to toss out all of my panties that I didn't feel amazing in and replace them with panties I only feel great in.

Now that I have your attention, let me explain . . . .

Like many people, I didn't give myself permission to only have things in my wardrobe that I felt great in, and even if I wanted to, I assumed my husband wouldn't be on board with it. It's not that he's a cheap guy, but growing up I had been programmed to believe that you keep things if they are still in good or decent condition.

Over the years that translated into me digging through my undergarments drawer, swimming through a sea of panties and settling on a pair that no one (but my husband) would see anyway. "Who cares what you wear underneath your clothes?" I'd tell myself to believe.

Looking through my drawer, seeing panties from 10 years ago that I had worn only a few times, that were still in new condition, subconsciously reminded me of how I used to feel in them. There was no way those cute little strings of delicate material would fit me now, but I kept holding on to the hope that I might be able to fit in them again "someday." I believed leaving them in my crowded panty drawer was the way to motivate myself to get back into the shape I had dreamed of for nearly a decade. Amidst the old, but still "new condition" panties were others, that though they fit me comfortably, were stretched and washed out; looking at them made me feel detached from my femininity. Sure, I had a few that were less than a year old, but they just didn't flatter my shape (they looked amazing on the model, but only seemed to enhance my imperfections).

I completely understood from my productivity and organizational training that if you didn't love something, then you were supposed to "lose it." But it wasn't until my Million Dollar Day that I started asking, "Does this inspire me? Does this energize or take away from me? Are there any negative feelings or memories attached to this?" And here was the kicker for my daunting panty selection: "Do I feel AMAZING in this?" I can honestly say, 95% of what was in that drawer did NOT inspire me, and I did NOT feel amazing wearing it.

I've adopted a new philosophy that anything that is not "me" anymore, is not empowering, or brings negative thought or energy, no longer has a home in my space.

I no longer settle on something that will just work, but I choose to wear what I'm in the mood for that day. It's an easy choice because everything in the drawer is inspiring. The result is that I feel amazing (dare I say, "sexy?"), no matter what I pull out of my drawer, which has brought about deeper intimacy in my marriage. (WOW, TMI?)

If you're not laughing with me yet, as I've divulged more than I'd ever have dreamed of in writing a book, this panty story is just part of the ripple effect that came from my Million Dollar Day.

Because of the Million Dollar Day, I now have an understanding of how the world's most productive, accomplished, high energy, high re-sults individuals do it. They move quickly. I mean FAST. Not crazy or feverish, but they move items requiring action out of their mental and physical real estate as though each of them were hot potatoes, enabling them to invite and be ready for the next thing.

The amount of things I process today surpass what I would do before in a week, and sometimes even in a month.

Perhaps what blew my mind the most during my Million Dollar Day were the amount of hours I was in focus during that 24-hour period. My husband and I moved forward what had been 140+ years of com-bined procrastination, creating new momentum in each of our things and to-do's. At midnight at the end of our long, focused day, I still had loads of energy to keep going if I had wanted.

Since that day, I went from knowing the productivity basics of what it takes to move something forward, like "What is the next step?" to now giving myself permission to quickly find one simple thing to move that to-do or project forward. And to quickly move on to the next thing. Things, tasks, projects, annoyances, sub-standards and to-do's are moved forward with speed that still amazes me. And it's simply because I have given myself permission to just focus on what I can do today to kick the ball forward with one simple action, without having to bring it to full completion. Simple actions that help me move forward include looking up a phone number, scheduling an appointment, or tossing out that item that has given me some kind of negative, un-serving energy to my environment.

When I think of this way of responding to ideas and to-do's, I can visualize a springboard; that when something comes in (through my inbox, from another person, or just a new thought in my mind), it immediately gets flung off the springboard to the first available thing to move it forward.

It created such a shift in my philosophy of what I keep in my life, it's almost as if my soul has been given permission with anything (physical, mental or emotional)—to move it forward without being attached to fully completing it, or to move it out of my life when I sense it is no longer serving my goals. The trickle effect has been nothing short of life changing.

My discovery of the Million Dollar Day and desperate need to be schooled on how to really make my life more efficient, productive and inspiring has been eye-opening. I've unveiled the core difference from the mainstream productivity stuff, which covers more of how to get more efficient with the workload you have, the processes, how to file things, the idea of making a decision the first time you touch a piece of paper, to love it or lose it, or to ask yourself "What's the next step?" The primary difference from mainstream productivity and philosophies from the MDD is that when you free up your mental and physical real estate from things that suck your energy and stagnate your momentum, you move your thoughts from the past into the future. This is where new relationships, business ideas, and flourishing comes from.

Christine Kominiak Results

The Dog Days Are Over: For 7 years we talked about finding a dog sitter or kennel that we would feel comfortable with leaving "our only child," our 70 pound red, floppy-eared Doberman Pinscher, so we could vacation with our family. During that time we held off on family trips because we didn't have a place to leave our dog. She had never spent a day away from people in her life and she had only stayed with family while we traveled. It's never a good feeling when your family goes on a trip but leaves one person behind because of the dog. Moving away from the family created even more of a logistical problem because now there was no family to leave her with. Since the MDD we have found a pet hotel that she has stayed at several times now. Our last trip was with our family to the Grand Canyon via a majestic, old steam engine. I'm relieved to know that come snow ski season, the whole family will be able to trek off to the snow, and our four-legged daughter will be happy while we're off skiing the slopes.

The Cancer Call: I was so glad that the MDD prompted me to reconnect with my best friend from High School. It had been 6 months since we had spoken, and I had intended on calling her more times than I could count. The problem is, the timing always seemed to be off. Reconnecting because of the MDD didn't seem like a big deal, until 3 months later I got a call from her as I was boarding a plane. She had cancer. I can only imagine how much more uncomfortable that call might have been, if it had been nearly a year at that point that we didn't speak. We talked about me coming to visit her during her treatments. My old self may have delayed, because of various reasons. But the "New Christine" knew the power of taking action to move things forward, especially for things that I know will be on my mind, consuming my mental real estate until I do something with them. After not seeing her for 2 years, I made the flight north to Portland in time to be with her during her last chemo treatment. It was a precious visit that I will never forget and always be glad I acted on. Since the MDD when I think of people I care about and want to connect with, I don't wait. If I can't do it that moment, I immediately set a reminder via my phone so that 6 months don't pass by before calling them.

Couples Massage: The day of my wedding I didn't realize what I was stepping into when I entered a spa for half a day of pampering and relaxation. I was injected with the dream bug of what it would be like to have regular days of pampering and relaxation like this with my loving groom. But the wedding came and went, and so did 10 years before the Million Dollar Day awakened my dream bug and opened both of us to everything we intended to be our reality. My husband didn't know until our MDD of this dream I had held down and inside for over a decade. It was almost as if the MDD gave us permission to make a fantasy a reality. Our MDD was on Saturday; we scheduled an appointment for the very next day, and shared our Sunday afternoon together embracing a whole new world of intimacy and relaxation together. Today monthly massages are a part of our emotional and physical health priorities.

The End: A surprising element of the MDD was moving forward or wiping away emotional baggage. During the course I was reminded once again of undone decisions about a friendship that went awry. Years had past since I learned there was a problem and that my friend was already long gone. But I still wondered about what words should be spoken. She had moved on with her life, and I thought I had moved on with mine. But I continued to be haunted by the dramatic dismount of what was my closest girl friend. What I didn't realize was, and just recently had my eyes opened by my husband, was that the doubts and questioning about what happened and what I should or shouldn't do or feel about it, were haunting me, keeping me from being open and engaging in new friendships. I was afraid I was going to get hurt and didn't want to open myself up for another blow. The MDD helped me to see how I could finally come to a decision one way or the other about it, so I could move on. That day I closed a chapter of my life that had been wrestling in my mind for 2 years. I have peace and am so relieved to be done with that conversation. I've opened myself up to new friendships and have a new perspective from the whole experience that makes me more mindful and engaged in my relationships.

Christine Kominiak's 5 Tips

#1- Get a partner (do it with your spouse, or get a friend to be there with you the whole day, they will help bring perspective and objectivity to help you plow through your list). Better yet, have them watch the MDD video with you. If you want them to fully get on board and have the vision of what's possible in this day, they will be a powerful support partner for you.

#2- Don't assume you know what the MDD is from reading this book or thinking it's just a to-do list. Watch the video all the way through; engage with it and write down the thoughts (even the tiniest, seemingly insignificant thoughts) popping in your head. Then, walk around your house (or your office) and note what annoys you or gives you any negative thought or energy.

#3- Give yourself permission to not bring everything on your list to completion because this day is about getting everything in your life that is undone into momentum. Though your focus is to knock off everything on your list in one day, open your mind to realize some things may take days or weeks to get done. The focus is to move everything on your list into momentum, so that it goes from being stagnant to alive and moving forward. You're simply kicking the ball forward on each item.

#4- The night before your MDD, review your MDD list and plot out time-specific activities. For example my MDD was in the middle of summer, so we planned ahead to knock out the outdoor items first before the sweltering heat kicked in.

#5- Journal at the end of your MDD. You'll forget the feeling, the freeing, the clarity, and your biggest take-aways if you don't write them down. Even looking back now at my journal, I can feel how I felt at the end of my MDD. Even still, I can reflect on how I've changed since then, and see areas that are worthy of re-implementing into my life again that I just didn't do long enough to make it a new habit.

About Christine Kominiak

Before Co-Founding LifestyleTrailblazers.com, Christine Kominiak co-authored "Insights On Productivity" and had an impressive 9 year career in home business direct sales, marketing, and productivity training. As a former "Life-By-Defaulter", Christine now works from wherever fuels her, with her husband, Matthew, together inspiring and empowering others how they can live their lives by design. The title, "Lifestyle Trailblazer" sums up Christine as an avid adventure seeker, fitness & health enthusiast, and intentional "live-er" of life!

Matthew Kominiak

When people ask me to sum up the Million Dollar Day, Matthew's story almost sounds too hype-filled to be real. And sometimes I resist sharing it, so that I do not appear too sensational.I will not steal his thunder...Well, maybe a little. :)

Here we go: His wife Christine (who also contributed an earlier chapter to this book) was born with essentially one deaf ear. As a child, she believed that it would always be a permanent part of her life. But inside the MDD video, I press hard (unrealistically hard) to itemize every facet of your health that you have been procrastinating on...and get new medical professions to rally for possible solutions to all our ailments. (HINT: there are many "healing-like" stories that come from people's MDD stories, but Christine's is one of the best).

In short, they called an ear specialist, and long story short, they fixed her hearing. I just sent them a text message and asked for an update. The reports are that her hearing deficiency is indeed healed. Music sounds fuller. Hanging out in crowded places isn't a lip-reading game anymore. And former communication problems between Matthew and Christine (which stemmed from her actual inability to hear some of what Matthew said, have been healed). It was a life-changing situation. And because they headed into their MDD with a radical focus, they received radical results. Over 93 items and a whopping 145 years of itemized procrastination was confronted in a single 24-hour marathon. Amazing.

If you think what I share with you here is amazing, wait until you experience his story first hand.

"Do we have hearing insurance?" Boy if I had a nickel for every time I heard that question; well . . . I'd have a nickel.

It was about 10 am on that beautiful June Saturday and my wife, Christine, and I were well over 4 hours into our Million Dollar Day. I was in my office at my desk, checking off yet another item on the list that represented over 140 years of the combined procrastination; we eliminated that day, when Christine walked in and asked that very question. Now you would think that a question like that, and the potential conversation to follow would easily throw a proverbial wrench into the finely tuned machine that was our Million Dollar Day. But that was not the case at all. In fact, I knew right where she was going.

You see, Christine was born with what the doctor called, a hereditary auditory affliction in her right ear. Or to put it simply, she couldn't hear very well in her right ear since she was born.

Though there was no physical pain, mentally it was debilitating. Especially when she discovered that if not treated by a certain age, there would be no way to reverse her condition. And the idea of never having normal hearing began to consume her daily thoughts, infecting them like a virus that swarms through your computer slowing it down and eventually grinding it to a complete stop.

What used to be just a passing thought, was becoming part of the identity of the person she saw every day in the mirror, unconsciously causing her to withdraw in social situations, or lash out in frustration. It was steering her on a course that would eventually change the very essence of who she is.
Now just picture in that moment, Christine standing in the doorway of my office, with a look of pure hope in her hazel eyes that was quietly shouting to the heavens, "I want to fix my ear!"

It was one of those moments in life, where time seemingly stood still, and as Christine sat down, preparing to plead her case, my first and only thought was . . . We can rebuild it, we have the technology.

Without a word, I swung over to the keyboard to consult with the Internet Jedi Master named Google. And in no time at all we had a discount hearing plan.

I gave her a number to call, "But it's Saturday; chances are they will not be there," she said. As I leaned back in my office chair with a sheepish grin, I reminded her that we just had to get the process started today.

So with a simple phone message, the first step of the journey to save her hearing was set in motion and another Million Dollar Day Victory with 14 years of procrastination wiped out.

We were first exposed to the Million Dollar Day, when I had received an email about an upcoming training from its creator and my mentor Mark Hoverson. Now any expert would agree, improving productivity and eliminating the paralyzing procrastination that keeps us all in check, is essential to success in life, love and business. So it was extremely ironic that the combined lack of productivity and the layers of procrastination that were miring my life at the time, was the very reason we did not attend the class.

Like so many people, we were constantly pressured with the ever growing weight of an ever growing "TO-DO" list in our lives and business. Daily tasks were taking months, if they got done at all. Every hour of everyday was consumed by trying to free ourselves from our endless struggles.

What used to be fun, free time together, that had once created precious life long memories, were now eternal stretches of uncomfortable silence. The reality was we were drowning in a sea of procrastination that was slowly poisoning our hearts, minds and our souls.

So when The Million Dollar Day became the headline training of the Internet Lifestyle Network apprentice membership, it was like being thrown a life preserver, so we could pull ourselves from the stormy sea that was our life.

This single DAY 'reset' our entire future. Our Million Dollar Day was an intoxicating cocktail of liberation and success, because in less than 24 hours Christine and I checked 93 items off our list, and renovated our mental real estate by eliminating exactly 145 years of lost productivity and procrastination from our lives.

Matthew Kominiak's Results

But hey, don't take my word for it, check out just a few of the things we were able to accomplish . . .

Financial Triage: Is your personal economy bleeding money? It turns out ours was, and we didn't even realize it. Imagine having a pin prick on the end of your finger. Of course it won't bleed a lot when you get it, but as you bump or move your finger, you open up the cut and it continues to bleed a little, delaying the healing. And that's what was happening with our finances. You see, a simple 20 minute review of our bank and credit card statements, revealed several monthly subscriptions we were no longer using or simply didn't need that were bleeding money from our bank account every single month. These items may only have been 10 or 20 dollar monthly fees, but I don't have to tell you, they can add up fast. Just think about it, your mind constantly bogged down wondering where did all the money go, keeping you from having that special something you desperately want in your life because you think you can't afford it. Is that any way to live? :(

Protecting our "A**ets": The last thing any entrepreneur (or anyone for that matter) wants, is to see everything they have worked for so hard for vanish in the blink of an eye. For years we convinced ourselves, that we would never fall victim to losing it all. But the reality was, this conversation was no longer just a passing thought . . . The idea of losing everything we had shed blood, sweat and tears over was beginning to haunt our dreams. We finally pulled the trigger to form a LLC that day, and all it took was a simple 2 minute IM chat to a friend to get the ball rolling. I felt like a 1000 lb weight was lifted from my shoulders, knowing we would not play a part in the horror story and legal battles that other people had to endure because they were not properly protected in business.

Taming The Paperless Tiger: It's true, email has a well deserved reputation for being a productivity killer. Like most people we had begun to neglect our email as we shifted to more instant communication methods. But every time I would hop on the computer, or check my smartphone, my inbox was angrily staring me right in the face. Imagine the feeling of dread that engulfs you seeing thousands of unopened messages, followed by the nagging question of . . . "What am I missing?" constantly percolating in your brain. Thoughts of missed opportunity, old friends, and family constantly distracting us back to our inbox, only to waste hours, adrift in a sea of spam. But in less than 60 seconds, we silenced those questions forever, by setting up a daily reminder on our calendar during our Million Dollar Day to encourage us to take 10 minutes to unsubscribe from email lists that did not serve us or our business. And in just a few short weeks we were finally able to bring peace and tranquility to our inbox.

The Time Freedom Formula: Everyone knows as a business owner, you can only grow your business so far without help. And for months I had an idea rattling around my brain that would help us expand our business, but I was worried that if I rocked the boat, our business may suffer. So when I put it on the Million Dollar Day list, I explained to Christine, I have to stop living letting this fear control me, and it was finally time to make a decision so we can move on. Obviously I didn't have to have the entire conversation figured out that day, or be prepared to make someone an offer. All I needed to do that day, was take the first step by sending a text message that opened the conversation. A conversation that led to the hiring of our first employee, opening up a new level of freedom in our lives. We were liberated from the chains that bound us, and for the first time in over a decade I felt like we had a business that no longer owned us.

The Solomon CEO Experience: This literally made our company over a million bucks, 1.5 Million to be exact. Now I know that sounds completely unrealistic, and to be honest I never expected this to happen either. You see, I had been through the Solomon CEO training, but Christine had yet to fully review it. So when it came up on the Million Dollar Day list, it only took a 5 minute conversation to set up an action plan to complete Solomon CEO cover to cover. Now, little did I know that this journey would uncover a gold mine of AH-HA moments. And the biggest of them all is when realized that all these years in business, I was asking the wrong question to my clients. Instead of "What can I do to help?", I started asking "What will make your job easier?" And it was this Gold Nugget that caused a massive shift in the way we communicated. One simple question separated us from the competition in the eyes of our clients that resulted in a financial windfall, and forever changed the way we run our business.

Extreme Garage Makeover: Now I can already hear you brain saying, "Do you really expect me to believe you redesigned up your entire garage?" And you are absolutely right. The fact is our garage was just in a state of clutter, like books just thrown in disarray on a book shelf. When you place them neatly on the shelf, the image projects a completely different energy than when they were just scattered about. You see every time we pulled the car into the garage we would take a mental picture of the jumble of boxes from our recent move that need to be broken down, and bins that were stacked incorrectly and that could topple at any moment. And these images were filling up our psychic ram and spiraling our minds into chaos. In reality it took a little over two hours to neatly arrange it all, but when we did it, we felt a tremendous metal release from a constant source of pressure and tension in our lives.

And this is just glimpse of the life changing experience of our Million Dollar Day.

So . . . you're probably wondering, What happened to Christine?

Well I'm happy to say that on November 12, 2013, Christine had Laser Stapedectomy (what we playfully refer to as the day she got her Bionic Ear).

Even though the end result took place several months later, one simple action was a catalyst of importance for the initial doctor's visit where Christine learned she was a candidate for surgery. The surgery that would relieve the side affects of her affliction that had been having negative impacts on her life.

Bottom line was it only took one quick phone call to finally put an end to the silent frustration that had defined her for years.

Now clearly you can see just how life changing The Million Dollars Day can be, but what does this all mean to you?

Well now that you are ready to experience your own Million Dollar Day, I would like to share with you our biggest takeaway and give you some helpful tips to help you embark on your journey and maximize your day.

First off, if you do nothing else, please burn this into your brain . . . Ready for it?

Nothing Is Off The Table!

This was huge for us. But I don't want devalue the importance of the little tasks, because like those little fees I mentioned above, they can add up fast. So when you are planning your Million Dollar Day, give yourself permission to ask your subconscious mind to dig deep. Allow yourself to drift back in time, and as you recall a memory something unfinished . . . no matter how big or small, write it on the list.

Starting now, you have permission to visualize your life without procrastination. And as each second of your Million Dollar Day ticks by you will begin to feel the liberation of silencing miniscule and mundane thoughts your brain has been wrestling with for years.

Matthew Kominiak's 3 Tips

#1- Watch The Training. You may think you have this all down, but be sure to completely watch the training video before you start, so you can be crystal clear on the process and eliminate the most procrastination.

#2- Write It Down. The pen is mightier than the sword and it's also mightier than the iPad. There is no better feeling victory when you physically check an item of a list when you have completed it.

#3- Get a Running Buddy. We are social creatures that love to see others triumph over adversity. So plan your Million Dollar Day with a friend or family member, so you can be there to celebrate the victories and help motivate one another through the day.

About Matthew Kominiak

Matthew Kominiak has an entrenched passion and excitement for entrepreneurialism. His light-hearted approach to business makes him a great mentor and strategist. Current co-founder of MCK Investment, LLC, a business development firm, he has been called "Psychologically
Unemployable" and is always ready to "Tee-Up" a round of gold.

He recently co-authored a life changing program, The Lifestyle Design Formula (lifestyletrailblazers.com/formula), teaching people how to stop living a life by default and start living a life by design today, no matter your present circumstances.
Matthew's incredible story of how he and his wife used this exact formula to liberate themselves from certain economic collapse and save their marriage from the brink of divorce. Through this simple 3-step process he was able to rediscover what was most important in his life and evaluate his level of physical and spiritual happiness to uncharted levels. Matthew takes complex issues of being an entrepreneur and makes them easy to understand and apply to your life.

Nearly two decades of running a multi-million dollar business from home allows him to combine real, practical wisdom with a unique insight to truly understand yourself, and gives you tools to open new opportunities and possibilities in your life.
Among some of Matthew's past and present business partners are David Bach, Mark Hoverson, Amstead, Amazon, and many other entrepreneurs and businesses worldwide.

Matthew's blog: lifestyletrailblazers.com/bio

Fusano Nagashima

Fusano privately shared with me her MDD story in tears. Of the thousands of reported MDD case studies, Fusano's story is one of the most profound, and sobering, stories I've heard. Again, my two big takeaways from her chapter are this:

#1- She relayed to me that when she walked into her deceased twin-sister's estate, she literally fell paralyzed to the ground. Fusano was in charge of closing out her sisters accounts, and settling the estate. The task was so overwhelming (nevermind the emotional pain of losing her sister) that it was very akin to having a panic attack. Fusano redeemed the event by using her MDD as a spark to be 100% ready to pass her estate easily and effortlessly to her family once she passes. It's a sobering story, but caused me to prep at extreme levels so that in the event of my untimely death, my wife and family and kids would have the least possible of logistical stress. It was a powerful experience.

#2- In her "tips" section, she recommends simply "avoiding procrastination" because the residual effect is not only increased stress, but lost money. The MDD tends to be a "creatively destructive" experience because it reboots our lives. Avoiding procrastination becomes easier after the day.

When I first learned about the Million Dollar Day through Internet Lifestyle Network (ILN) it was some time after the death of my twin sister. It was just around the time when I started to feel that I must clear out my twin sister's estate and I shouldn't procrastinate it any longer.

I lost my twin sister on August 13, 2012. She was suffering from colorectal cancer for 4 years. I had to watch her struggle with pains and difficulties. The only thing that I felt we were lucky in was our strong belief and faith in God; we believed He could make things better. We went through all the hard times with praying. There was a time where she wasn't able to talk, write, and walk, but because of her strong faith in God, she recovered from those situations.

Her death discouraged me a lot and I couldn't touch her possessions for a long time, but a ton of things were waiting.

I could no longer stay in tears and extend what I had to do. I had to start. But it was way too much and I couldn't figure out what to do.

I started to list up things I had to do.

First, I had to collect all of the official certificates, like certificate of detailed family lines, certificate of birth and death, and domicile address. They had to cover not only my twin sister, but the whole late family and those of us who were living. It seemed endless. It took about a month to just collect all the necessary information since I couldn't get them in one place. I started to make reports to official places on various things that I had to.

It took about 10 months for me after her death to start clearing out her possessions at her estate since I, myself, had to be in the hospital for the operation with her. The first thing I had to do was pull everything out of her drawers, storage, cupboards, and closets.

It was beyond any of my expectations how much time I had to spend on this first step. It was also more than I imagined it would be emotionally. It seemed that all my strength failed. I was unable to move.

There were things that had been stored throughout the years of my parents and my twin sister, and some of them were mine. All of them had their own histories. Clearing out of her possessions—clothes, grocery, medical care equipment, shoes, kitchen wares, stationeries, bags, books, albums, furniture—everything in her estate had to be collected. I was lucky to be able to do this with my younger sister.

It was not easy to decide what to keep. I wanted to keep some, but I knew they wouldn't make me happy, so I decided to keep only one thing . . . that was her bible. Once I decided what to keep, it made it easier to see what to do next. I got garbage bags and me and my younger sister started to put everything in bags without thinking like a machine. Once we started, it became just one less thing to do. I tried not to dwell in the memories of past.

There were 2 things that were most difficult for me and I needed time to think about them.

Fusano Nagashima's Results

Albums: There was a ton of albums of me and my twin sister in our childhood years with our parents. There were some photos that I saw for the first time.

We have double mothers. The real mother gave us life, and our second mother actually took care of us. We didn't see our real mother for 30+ years after she left us when we were 3 years old, so we've never seen any photos of us from when we were 1 to 3 years old. Our real mother had them and she sent them later to my twin sister. It was emotionally difficult and I couldn't stand up for hours when I saw them.

When I first met our real mother, I couldn't call her "mother", and I still cannot since I felt guilty to our second mother who actually took care of us. I know there was some conflict between them, but the only thing that matters to me is that I'm here because of everything that had happened in the past.

It's always difficult to go back to the past that gives us emotional baggage.

The photos were old monochrome and that made me discouraged. I couldn't touch them for days and I didn't go to my sister's house for a while. It was too difficult for me to be there, but I had to push myself.

I decided to take the photos and scan them to preserve them digitally. The old monochrome photos had too much history and emotion, but the digital photos didn't garner the same feelings. However, I just didn't have the energy to do so and I was unwilling to do anything for a while.

After some time had passed and I had managed to convert all the photos to digital and disposed all the old albums of our childhood, something started to happen. I started to feel energy coming back and that energy was stronger than before.

I could finally accept the fact of my twin sister's death and our past. This became the start of moving forward. It gave me power, and at the same time it cleared my mind and made me want to do more things. I know she's no longer here on Earth, but she remains in my heart.

I started to travel a lot. I went with my husband to Malaysia (3 times), Hong Kong, Canada in 2013, and in 2014 to Vietnam, Singapore, Malaysia (4 times) with my husband and to USA (3 times) by myself. The trip to San Diego in April 2014 was the foundation for me to do ILN. I feel I'm with my twin sister wherever I go. We work together.

Credit cards, membership cards, bank cards: I had to do more detailed and complicated things related to her personal belongings like credit cards, membership cards, insurance, and bank cards.

I had to contact all of them and cancel them. I needed official certificates for that purpose. She had a lots of cards . . . And I am the same way.

When I learned about the Million Dollar Day through ILN I was wondering what Million Dollar Day meant. I was told that a Million Dollar Day is supposed to give us a powerful mindset shift and make us prepare for our next level by getting rid of procrastination and help eliminate the emotional baggage that we have. But I still did not get what it exactly meant until I did it. It was not clear to me how the words "Million Dollar Day" connected to the things we needed to do, but now it's clear.

Going through things I had to face after the death of my twin sister, it made me think something and it was a huge question for me.

What would happen to my children if I died tomorrow? They don't know anything about my personal status like financial status or credit card status. What would happen if I ended up in debt or had to take out a loan? What about all of my membership cards or online business transactions that have to be done online? How would they stop and cancel them? I have to prepare for my death for my family. If not, they will be left with all struggles that I had to go through after my twin sister's death. It's a tough thing. I need to make it simpler for them. There're people my age who don't use the Internet, and in that case it might be easier for their families, but I use online transactions in many ways.
I realized recently that online transactions had a distinctive feature. It's easy to start things online, but it takes time, needs more attention and energy to close them. I know some families cannot touch, for example, all of their recently deceased member's property because of things they cannot find or they don't know. I found also that we needed to have certain knowledge about legal transactions as well. It's not common for many people here in Japan to have personal consultants like in Western countries, so we have to think about our children ourselves.

Million Dollar Days shed a light on my past and helped me accept the facts in front of me. It gave me the energy to go forward, and last, but not least, it clearly showed me what to do before I leave this Earth.

My Million Dollar Days will continue . . .

Fusano Nagashima's 5 Tips

#1- Let's not have the wrong illusion that we may use things in the future.

#2- Let's always have space for something. Organizing is not enough. Space is important. It affects your mental capacity.

#3- Let's avoid procrastination. It will waste your time. How much time are you wasting searching for something? Time is money. Saving time means saving money.

#4- Let's make a list and make a routine to clean things each day, week, or month.

#5- Let's be prepared for death for our children. It's going to happen. Make it simpler and easier for our family to organize things after our death.

About Fusano Nagashima

Entrepreneur. Online Marketer. Traveller. Believer in God

Fusano has the passion for encouraging people to have 2nd income stream line and live a life, and not live for life. It's not only for an unseen future, but also to prepare for the retired life.

She loves traveling—that was her dream. She lives in Tokyo, Japan and Kuala Lumpur, Malaysia. She enjoyed visiting more than 15 countries. Her long term 9-5 job, the network business and online business helped her achieve her dreams.

Facebook: facebook.com/fusano.nagashima

Jaden Easton

I call Jaden the "Lebron James" of the internet. Lebron never went to college to play basketball. He just went straight to the NBA and became a top champion almost immediately.

Similarly, Jaden never went to college, because while still in high school, he generated $500,000 online through his blogging. Today, he is one of my partners. And I love him like a son. Two pieces of intel I love about his chapter are:

#1- He totally "detoxed" his work environment. He ended up with 6 30-gallon trash bags of stuff removed from his creative space. Immediately, he felt fresher and like the next level of prosperity was right around the corner for him. In less than a year, he relocated to Thailand for an entrepreneurial excursion and earned $20,000 in one week from his first information product.

#2- This will sound insane because it is, but one night, I had a vision-like experience, and saw Jaden approaching me to bring one of my quiet projects into prominence. Within six months, Jaden asked if he could stay at our house for a live event I was hosting, and a few hours before he was scheduled to hop on a plane back to Thailand, he said very timidly, "Mark, I see how you run your businesses and family, and I want to quit everything and help you build the dream." With zero negotiation (the only promise is that I wouldn't pay him), he began an apprenticeship. Six months later I actually started paying him. And he has become, literally, an answer to my dreams. Thank you Jaden. Enjoy his story.

I was 19 years old, living in my parents' house, feeling bogged down, my finances were going downhill and in a way I felt trapped. Trapped both mentally and physically from all the clutter around me, holding me down like an anchor. It was impacting my business, my productivity my happiness and was preventing me from grasping an opportunity to travel to Thailand.

I heard about the Million Dollar Day at a time in my life when I needed it most. It was at a time where my online technology news business was collapsing after having previously done $500,000 the year prior, I owed tens of thousands of dollars to the government in taxes which I hadn't anticipated and I was barely earning enough income to scrape by month-to-month.

It's safe to say life was chaotic and as unorganized as could be, I needed a way to re-take control of my life and get back on track but I had absolutely no clue where to start. All of this put me in a state of constant anxiety, anger, frustration and was the closest I have been to rock bottom.

The Million Dollar Day was a godsend for me. It was on this day that I had the belief in myself reinstated that I was capable of turning things around. I had finally reached a point where not doing something was more painful than actually going to the effort to do what needed to be done to resuscitate both my life and business.

So I took what I learned from the Million Dollar Day and spent the next few hours mapping out everything that was keeping me stuck in place, like being trapped in quicksand, making my life stagnant, and preventing growth. I wanted to ensure this was going to be the most productive day in my life, because it was from this point forward I was going to be putting my foot down. I knew it wasn't going to be easy, but more importantly I knew an above average life requires an above average amount of effort.

Jaden Easton's Results

Work Environment Detox: The first thing I set out to do was to clean my working environment, which at the time was also my bedroom in my parents' house. Over the years I had accumulated so much clutter which filled my desk drawers with, under my bed and in my closet. This was a mixture of old school work, toys/knick-knacks from when I was younger, old clothes which no longer fit me and made me feel disempowered and outdated technology I no longer needed.

So I went on a total room detox and filled about six 30-gallon trash bags with things that I no longer needed. For the first time ever, my room actually looked empty ready to invite wealth and prosperity instead of rejecting it. All around me were only things that empowered me and were conducive to a productive working environment.

Discovered Untapped Wealth: After having detoxed my room, I had identified a bunch of things which I could actually sell to make some additional money to support my trip to Thailand. This included things like an old camera, iPods and other technology accessories I had been sent previously to do reviews on, my old Windows computer which was still in top-notch condition yet I never used since upgrading to a Mac, aftermarket car parts and more!

So what I did right then and there was take pictures of everything I no longer needed and created classified postings on Craigslist for each item. After about a week I was able to make $3,350 after everything was sold. The funny thing was, without doing the Million Dollar Day I would have never known I had so much untapped wealth just sitting not being utilized.

Uncluttering My Digital Reality: Next up on the roster was getting my digital reality in check. All of my business is done online, so my computer is one of the main "oxen" of my business and since my computer was in just as bad as a state as my room originally was I once again felt my brief sense of once again being in control fade away. My inbox had over 6,000 emails, which would constantly result in me missing important emails and caused unacceptable response times getting back to people. Finding files on my desktop was a chore as it resulted in me searching through a labyrinth of files, most of which I no longer needed because they were from old projects.

So not only did I clear out my entire email inbox, I almost wiped out my entire hard drive and only kept files relating to current projects and went a step further by organizing them the right way using various folders segmenting everything into their proper categories. This not only made my computer faster, but dramatically increased my productivity because it no longer meant I needed to spend time searching for what I was looking for.

I would say all of this unorganization in my digital world cost me roughly an hour of wasted time per day, whether it was from searching for files, digging through emails, having my computer freeze etc. If you put a price on your time of just $30/hour and expand that over 2 years, which was about the time my computer was in this chaotic state that would mean a loss of $15,600 (working 10 hours, 5 days a week). Can you imagine the loss if I continued this for 10 years? That would be a loss of $78,000. And the sad thing is the majority of people will continue working in an unproductive environment their whole life (and their dollars per hour is much higher).

Identified Unnecessary Business Expenses: I additionally decided to go over my business expenses to identify areas which I could reduce costs, and was surprised to find I had close to $400 a month coming out of services which I was no longer using which ranged from marketing tools to subscriptions to various membership sites. I added it up and realized that these services were recurring for almost a year, which means I had saved myself $4,800 in unnecessary expenses year-to-year by canceling them all.

Created New Roadmap: The last step of my Million Dollar Day was to come up with a game-plan of how I was going to get my business back on track. Part of this involved moving out to Thailand to place myself in a completely different atmosphere and the other part was I was going to craft for Mark Hoverson, an internet marketing mogul who's generated millions of dollars online. What impressed me about Mark though is that he wasn't only successful in business but in life as well. He had a great marriage/family life, was very well off financially and still had a great quality of life. I knew that if I was going to model myself after something it was going to be him.

About a year later after coming up with this game plan during my Million Dollar Day I moved to Thailand for 4 months, built an affiliate marketing team of 300 people, released an info product teaching people how to build a business online which grossed nearly $20,000 the 3 days and was able to relocate to Arizona thanks to an opportunity to apprentice alongside Mark Hoverson.

All of this was because on this one day, which resulted in me wiping out close to 60 years of procrastination, gave me the second wind I needed to do everything needed to be done in order to get my life and business back on track. Since my Million Dollar Day my future has never looked brighter and I'm actually excited for the years to come instead of dreading what the next day will hold.

Jaden Easton's 5 Tips

#1- Wake up early and get a start on the day because today's different. You want to set the tone that from this day forward everything changes, and how can that be if you repeat the same daily schedule as every other day? Set your alarm clock earlier than usual, and aim to give yourself 20 hours to dedicate to solely your Million Dollar Day.

#2- Set the intention before you start your Million Dollar Day of how this day is going to forever alter your life. For me I imagined that after completing my Million Dollar Day I was going to no longer wake up dreading the day, I was going to wake up full of energy. I imagined that I would actually be working less because I would be more productive and that no longer would I place success far off in the distance. Instead I would enjoy the journey. And sure enough all of this became a reality very shortly after completing my Million Dollar Day because I set that initial intention.

#3- Spend time creating your Million Dollar Day List, don't rush through this step. Make it as thorough as possible and strive to fill it with more things than you think you are capable of finishing in the day because you're going to surprise yourself at how much you can accomplish.

#4- Once you create your Million Dollar Day list based off the intentions you set to begin with, prioritize your list and knock off your highest leverage activities first. To identify your highest leverage activities ask yourself if you could only do one thing on that list all day long, what would it be? Ask yourself the same question again to figure out your second and third highest-leverage activities.

#5- Have an MDD BIG so you have some kind of accountability. In the College Fraternity world your BIG is someone who looks after you and has your back, someone who keeps you aligned with what needs to be done. Whether it's a spouse, a family member or a friend find someone which you can share what you're about to be doing and have them check in on you once or twice throughout the day to share your progress so far and re-motivate your to make this your most productive day ever.

About Jaden Easton

Jaden Easton is an adventupreneur, fitness enthusiast and visionary. Jaden teaches other entrepreneurs and small business owners, how to manifest their definition of lifestyle design through the power of the internet and direct response marketing.

In High School Jaden founded a blog which generated over $500,000. Since then he's used both his successes and failures as a catalyst towards progressing his life, business and the lives of others through his coaching/mentoring programs, information products and free content available at his social media channels.

Follow Jaden's journey over at: jadeneaston.com

Jamie Waters

Jamie Waters is a man from the United Kingdom and has an almost unnerving integrity. Having visited with him privately on several occasions, his conversation has the dry wit and a refreshingly un-American ability to communicate without the glaze of worrying about political correctness in every breath.

His attention to systematic thinking combined with genuine care for people is unique, as and is the power of his entrepreneurial prowess. The two biggies that popped out to me in his story are:

#1- His understanding of the physic stronghold his long overdue un-erased whiteboard had on his life. In short, for nearly four years, he left his record-high revenue numbers on his whiteboard. Like an old trophy, seeing those numbers written did not inspire him anymore, they actually reminded him of "the good old days" when money flowed like wine. Just the act of erasing them on his MDD opened up a new future. This is the quintessential purpose of the MDD. Physically removing those pen markings from his visual landscape gave him a renewed freedom to create bigger results (which he quickly went on to do).

#2- Jamie details the "small wins", which are actually huge wins. Our financial lives can be likened to a bucket, the little leaks (left unfixed) continue to drain money and cause us to waste a portion of our income just to pass it through the leaked buckets. His notes on small stuff like changing dentists, changing his post code, finding uncashed checks hidden amongst the clutter…stuff like that basically fills in the holes and gives us a bucket prepared to receive money without loss. The next few pages are excellent.

Like many entrepreneurs I had a whiteboard which allowed me to keep track of appointments, artwork deadlines, delivery dates and ideas for growth. Only one problem, the information was 4 years out of date. 2008 was the first full year after graduating from University. Going from being a broke student to making around $3,500 a month was like winning the lottery. I got my first car. I moved out of the family home. Clients were joining the waiting list like people queue for the latest iPhone.

Unfortunately, just like most small businesses around that time, that thing called the global recession hit. Most people think that the first and easiest thing to cut in a budget is advertising. Naturally I would disagree, and so did my balance sheet. One by one customers stopped paying their bills and year after year things get progressively more difficult.

Looking back, holding onto the memories of that year, the most successful and exciting of my life, is probably what was holding me back. Stopping me from growing and moving into a space of being able to help more people than just myself. The MDD allowed me to accept and let go of the past, creating the space in my life for what would be a very interesting next 12 months.

The moment I took the cleaner spray and wiped it away I realized I was instantly opening up the future. Opening up new frontiers like the trailblazers of the past. The experience of the last 4 years, the victories and the losses felt that it came to this moment. It was like a restart of the journey for me, but starting from a higher position.

Back in 2008, with the generous help of my family, I purchased a local offline advertising company. It was my first venture into entrepreneurship, I was young, excitable, impressionable and up to that point, 2008 was the most exciting and successful of my life.

Fast forward to 2011 things and things were going downhill. One by one clients stopped paying their bills and things got harder, almost to breaking point.

By wiping the whiteboard, by removing the visual reminders of the successful meetings, appointments, artwork deadlines, delivery dates - it was like letting go of the past. I was acknowledging the glory year was over and forcing myself to look again to the future.

I had already made the decision that I needed something else, something to supplement the income and a friend showed me what Network Marketing and more recently Affiliate Marketing, had to offer.

That journey was not initially easy. I lost money in 'deals'. I jumped around from one thing to another like a cat on a hot roof trying to find an easy way to safety. Even today business is still challenging so at the time of doing my MDD while I knew things had improved, I had no idea the direction my life would go at the time of writing this chapter. It takes a special type of person to be honest with themselves, you know, that type of honesty that requires you to look deep inside you and wrestle with your inner consciousness. While at the time I did not realize the significance of what the simple 4-year-old whiteboard represented, looking back it took a lot of effort to add it to the list and clean it. Even when going through the initial drafts of this book with my fellow authors, I was sat at the back of the room thinking how 'lame' writing a chapter about a whiteboard was. Amazon best seller? Yea right.

But we all have a whiteboard in our life.

We all have the ghosts that, for the best of unconscious reasons, we are holding on to. Most of the time this turns out to be sentimental thoughts linking with a small real world object like a portal to another dimension. Think the TV show Hoarders but inside your mind.

Only when we acknowledge the weight of the past is keeping us there, can we purge it from our lives. Once purged we can invite the new, the exciting and the more successful that on every level is vastly superior.

Would I be where I am today, in a position to help tens of thousands of people on a daily basis if my wall planner still said 2008?

I very much doubt it.

Jamie Waters' Results

18 Months: From a previous business I used 2 freephone numbers and cancel mobile broadband and freephone numbers costing £45 a month over the period we Wasting £810 . Enough to pay for my new Mac-Book Pro, approx. $1,300.

2 years: There was a light under the kitchen worktop that had not worked for 2 years, each time I went to prepare a meal for friends or family, I had to turn on different lights.

6 months: I purchased a new heart rate monitor to help with my fitness training. Setup heart rate monitor with PC—6 months. As a football (soccer) referee we are required to train regularly and maintain a certain level of fitness and training with a heart rate monitor allows you to do that so much easier by training within heart rate zones. A 10-minute process that I'd been putting off for about 6 months let me have more confidence when training, which in turn makes me a fitter, more confident match official.

6 months: The majority of online companies pay their commissions in USD and after being charged pretty high exchange rates I finally contacted the bank to setup a USD account that I could be paid directly into. The amount of money I have saved on fees is incalculable. By making it easier to invite money into my life, it has the natural effect of actually bringing more money into my life.

2 years: Moving dentist: Since moving to Holmfirth from my home town of Dewsbury, there were a lot of things I put off. The average person moves 5 times in their lifetime, one of the most annoying things is needing to update your address with different people. Banks, Utilities, even the supermarket loyalty card (I once knew of a friend who didn't update their address for 5 years, only to find the ex-wife was spending their points on the cardholder's behalf!). So for the next 2 years, while driving past the local one twice a year I wasted 45mins each way, money spent on fuel and endured horrendous traffic. Not being a big fan of the dentist, it now feels like I'm visiting the spa, rather than a sterile danger zone!

12 months, booking a blood donation: In England the slogan to entice people to donate is 'Save a life, give blood'—yet for 12 months I continually put this off. To say I could have saved 4 lives in that time might sound a bit grandiose, but it did make me feel guilty. If that is something you've been putting off—add it to your MDD list now and save a life. Something different, yet elegantly simple.

1 month, order ink for printer: I wasn't able to print for 1 month!

2 months: Tidied the tables under the desk. At the time of doing my first MDD, I had moved into a new apartment. We know the value of having a neat and tidy workspace, but not many of us think about the space under our desks. Clearing this clutter and mental energy resulted in a huge sense of wellbeing and is something I would hugely recommend. So grab those ties and get hiding those cables!

5 months: $60 in unopened cheques found and banked. Cutting this one fine, cheques only have a lifespan of 6 months before they expire and need to be re-written.

3 months: Clean the bins. In our new place the wheelybins (garbage cans) are close to the road, we walk past them every time we walk into the house. After three months I finally arranged to have them professionally cleaned inside and out. You might laugh, but something as simple as this frees up a tiny part of the mind to focus on something else!

Jamie Waters' 5 Tips

#1- Do be honest with what you need to do. This will allow you to truly go through every little thing that is holding you back.

#2- Do let people know not to contact you. Turn off your phone, Skype and Facebook—This will allow you to concentrate on your entire list without distractions.

#3- Do be disciplined, work through the list one by one, rather than part of each point here and there. The concentration and focus will make you more productive.

#4- Do be sensible about the order of each task on the list—have smaller jobs at the top of the list, then some that might take a while. This will give some small 'wins' first giving instant gratification.

#5- Don't get distracted. I cannot stress the importance of this. All too often we flit from one thing to another and actually find we never get anything done. If something comes up while working on a task, add it to the bottom of the list. Staying on point is by far the best way to ensure maximum productivity.

About Jamie Waters

 Jamie lives in the small beautiful village of Holmfirth in West Yorkshire, England. An avid sports fan, Jamie is a football (soccer) referee and officiates in both the professional and semi-professional game. Being and online entrepreneur, Jamie loves to travel and meet new people while sampling new cultures and experiences.

Kristi Carter

Where do I begin with the magnanimous aura that is linked to Kristi? She is warm and funny and kind and creative and interesting and more. When people ask me about the power of the MDD, I rarely do not tell her tale.

Here's the two "aha-moments" I took from her story:

#1- Have you heard the old wives tale about how ancient jungle people used to capture monkeys? I don't know if it's true, but it's said that they would place a banana inside an anchored jar of some sort. When the monkey detected the luscious fruit, it would reach it's hand in the jar and grab the banana. However, once they made a fist around the fruit, they would be unable to pull their hand out of the jar. When the captures arrived, the monkey would refuse to let go of the fruit (which would in turn allow their hand to slip out of the jar). Because they would not let go, they were easily captured. As entrepreneurs, we often do the same thing. Kristi invested $20,000 of her hard-earned savings into a much-cherished business idea. But the idea didn't take off. So for 10 years, she had stacks upon stacks of inventory in her garage, staring her in the face EVERYDAY she parked her car. As the boxes dilapidated, she sort of "held on" that maybe someday she'd revive the idea. It was a block to all her new ideas (plus a huge space-eater in her garage).

#2- But on her MDD, she chose to clear that space completely. But instead of throwing it away, she donated it to a cancer society. The society redeemed the inventory and put it to good use. It's an amazing story of redemption. Plus, with the past behind her, the clouds parted and new business ideas emerged immediately. It's everything the MDD represents. Enjoy the next few pages.

I heard about the Million Dollar Day two years ago during Mark's first MDD webinar. What he said on the video was compelling, insightful and heartfelt. His message was clear: Your life will change by cleaning up your 'Life'. The steps seemed simple to apply and said to myself that 'someday' I will do my Million Dollar Day. That was two painful years ago of painful struggles with debt and possible failure of my fledgling business. My house started piling up with clutter and junk. Not even a quarter of all the items in my house were ever used. I compensated by telling myself I would declutter once my business was successfully launched. But my business was growing at a painfully slow speed due to my lack of technical knowledge. I began to get depressed, and I had a gnawing, unhappy feeling overall which is unusual since I am generally an upbeat, happy person. The threat of failure caused my confidence to wane. I had no place to turn. I figured that there was nothing to lose by doing the Million Dollar Day . . . so I finally did it.

In the year 2000, I was a very happy newlywed. Offsetting this euphoria, was an extreme dislike of working under the rule of my Silicon Valley boss in the landscape business. Although I was the top sales and marketing person, I hated how I was treated. I felt unappreciated. I knew the solution was to start my own business.

I have always been creative and artistic. Several of my paintings and photographs decorate the walls of my house as well as my friends and families homes. I also study cooking from many exotic countries. I have frequent dinner parties to tantalize my friends or families palettes. Coming up with new ideas is easy for me. Anxious to start my new business, I came up with the idea of supplying restaurants and hotels with beautiful plastic fruits or vegetables packed in large glass decorative round jars sealed with red plastic, wrapped in raffia. So, I got to work and created a company called Jar Art. I had visions of seeing them in all the Chilies Restaurants throughout the country.

I enthusiastically made dozens of prototypes, designed a brochure and bought lots of inventory. Over the next few years I sold a whopping 25 jars despite having a $20,000 inventory stored in my garage. What went wrong? I found that it can be difficult starting a business even with a good idea. I was hesitant asking investors for money, doing trade shows, and unsure how to ramp up profitably. So the expensive boxes of inventory sat and started rotting in my garage. The one store that did carry Jar Art went out of business. I then became more interested in online business and lost interest in Jar Art. This was the end of my first business, Jar Art, but I still had a ton of Jar Art pieces taking up room in my garage.

Every time I went to get into my car I would glance at those boxes and feel like a failure. The cheap, Chinese cardboard boxes were starting to bend, melt from dampness and fall apart. The fruit colors were fading. I thought that I would eventually get back to that business once my online business was going smoothly. However, I realized that years were going by and my garage was still a mess. It was painful watching $20,000 of inventory sit and rot. It paralyzed me. It wanted to get rid of it, but it cost me so much. Solution: I put this item on my Million Dollar Day 'to-do' list.

It felt liberating to make the call to the Cancer Society. They picked up all those slumping boxes of glass jars and plastic fruits to take to their store to sell. End Result: The Cancer Society will sell the fruits and jars receive approximately $10,000 for that inventory. A win-win for everyone. It is a win for me because, I learned valuable lessons about starting a business. Plus, I cleaned out my garage which made it much more pleasant to get into my car. I was relieved to chalk this business experience up in my life and move on. It's a win to the Cancer Society because my donation will help an extremely worthy cause.

By doing my MMD and disposing of 50 boxes of lingering inventory, I was able to let go of that self-doubt and feeling of failure. In reflection, this was actually a positive learning experience about business. Because of all these boxes cluttering up my garage. I realized that I never, ever want to have a business that requires physical storage. Now my online business has no inventory and my garage is clean. Hurray!

All you have to do is watch Mark's video, write everything down that you have been putting off, how long you have been thinking about it, schedule a day for it to be done, then do it. Do not deceive yourself into thinking that you know how to do this without watching Mark's video and following the exact steps. The video will give you tips and insight about the Million Dollar Day that you may not expect. Once you do your first Million Dollar Day watch your life explode with opportunities!

Kristi Carter's Results

The ideas for a new book came into mind: The day after my MDD the new book outline was done. The Title of my new book is: The Elysian Fields. The book is a science fiction novel set in the year 2050. It is about a society where people must have a license in order to start a family. The preface is that bringing children into the world is the biggest responsibility for both families and societies to behold.
In order to obtain the license a couple must be mentally, financially, physically and spiritually prepared to have a family. If couples do not meet these criteria, they are required to go through stringent self-development classes until they are ready to provide a good foundation for a child. The end results in this society are both positive and negative. The positive attributes are: no poverty, disease, deformities or mental illness exists.

The Government has no welfare system, because it doesn't need one. All the citizens are healthy, happy and productive. New technology is being invented exponentially benefitting everyone. The planet's ecosystem is in balance due to no pollution or overpopulation. The negative attributes is that the rebels think this license system is archaic and evil. The few couples who are denied the license are creating their own cults against the Standard. There are grumblings of a war about to start.

Eliminated a fire hazard in my office: The accumulation of 20 years of family/life photos piling up near electrical outlets, I could smell something burning as I worked occasionally. Now I knew why! Result: boxed up those photos to be put into a photo album.

I got a massage on my MDD which made me feel like a million bucks: I've been thinking about getting a massage for two whole years! I just kept putting it off. Thank goodness I decided that it was an important thing to put on my MDD. My body felt aligned, whole, healthy and energized. I have more energy for my business and personal life.

I made phone calls to my doctor to set up a general check up, eye check up and skin scan: This could add years to my life. Little did I know my doctor set up his own practice and is in high demand. Thank goodness my insurance still covers the health costs. Because of the high demand for this doctor, I had to wait for 3 months to have my appointment. I have peace of mind knowing that I am still covered by my health insurance and I have an appointment with one of the best doctors in California.

I now do things I have been putting off more readily and quickly: I quickly clean up the spills in the refrigerator instead of letting them sit there for months and stain my white refrigerator. Or I clean out a drawer without thinking too much about it. I just get it done. Doing even these stupid, simple things made me feel more capable and in control of my life. The tension of putting off little things has made me feel empowered. I am no longer a prisoner to procrastination. I have more self respect and determination to complete my goals in life, no matter how big they might be.

Kristi Carter's 5 Tips

#1- Do not go through the day frantically.

#2- Go through your list methodically and thoroughly.

#3- Feel the feeling of completion.

#4- Enjoy the process of letting go. This may be emotionally letting go of the memories attached to those old items.

#5- Allow the new clear space in your mind/psyche to entertain new goals and ideas you've been putting off.

About Kristi Carter

Kristi Carter lives in Northern California with her husband, surrounded by her beautiful garden. She is an avid tennis player, world traveler and lover of knowledge. Kristi has developed several creative companies. Some call her a visionary. If you give her a problem, she will quickly provide the solution. She has a knack for predicting what the marketplace needs in terms of mindset and know how. She has struggled to learn the new technology, yet it is a passion for Kristi because she sees the internet future is the new frontier. She has studied under various online business professionals, all offering different aspects of online businesses. With all of her internet marketing study she and Jay Conrad Levinson published her first book, Guerrilla Marketing to Baby Boomers.

Kristi is currently in the process of starting a movement to empower Baby Boomers to get over the fear of technology so they too can enjoy the freedom of working online.

Laurie Conrod

When we were first talking about the idea of making the MDD into a book, Laurie said with total conviction, "Mark, this idea could put you on Oprah."

Whether or not her prophesy materializes, her words startled me into bigger thinking. She was in the original community of early MDD-experimenters. And she witnessed first-hand the life-altering effects this process was having on people. Laurie has a gift of inspiring and encouragement. It's heavily impacted the view I have of myself. And I will always thank Laurie for her years of teaching me to recognize the value of my work. She's been a godsend to me. Thank you Laurie.

Because now I'm running out of page real estate to share two big take-aways from her story, I will sum it up with this one big monster point:

#1- Laurie's daughter brought her a beautiful glass necklace from a long-ago trip to Venice, Italy. Amongst the busyness of everyday life, the necklace went missing…for 8 YEARS!

Laurie told me prior to her MDD that her ultimate goal was to hopefully rediscover the treasured piece of jewelry her daughter gave her. Well, on her MDD day: she struck gold, or shall we say "glass", she found the necklace and with great satisfaction relayed the message to me.

It was like finding sunken treasure. The MDD creates that feeling over and over. Lost items appear. This is the restorative power of doing an MDD with vigor. Laurie's story is dear to my heart. Enjoy her share it in her own words.

I was excited to tackle my list because I was excited for my move from Connecticut to California. The only reason I was NOT overwhelmed, was because of the wisdom I gained from the MDD training.

I knew Mark when he first released the MDD training, and it resonated with me instantly because I'm so good at putting things off even though I have them on my mind, weighing me down. So after I watched the training I did several mini-million dollar days, and felt relief, clarity and renewal. But when I did the MDD this time, it was in conjunction with a pending move cross-country. It was perfect timing for me to embrace the MDD again, because I had to make big decisions about what was most important to me to keep in my life, and what I could let go of.

My MDD wasn't just about cleaning drawers and closets, throwing things out, and putting stuff back in closets in an orderly fashion. The MDD helped me make crucial, gut-wrenching decisions, because the training gave me the deeper meaning of what serves me and what doesn't, so I could make the big move cross-country and not take a lot of baggage with me (pun intended) to start my new life. After a MDD, you really do have a new life.
Imagine knowing where everything is in your house. Every closet is clean, orderly, and only the things that really matter to you are in them. Every drawer, cupboard, the basement, the garage, are all organized and nothing is lost.

In fact, you've discovered precious possessions that have been lost for years. You've rediscovered precious pictures that have been stored away for years, special trinkets that have been passed down in your family, each one with its own unique story.

Imagine giving keepsakes to your friends and family now, so they know you wanted them to have them. These are some of the experiences I've had with the MDD.

It sounds cliché, but you have to experience a MDD to believe it. It's one thing to clean some drawers and closets, we all do that here and there. A MDD is much deeper and bigger than that. My MDD opened me up to thinking at a higher level because I let go of the psychological burden of material possessions routed in the past. I let go of papers, objects, paraphernalia and pictures that brought up bad memories. Getting rid of all that stuff made me feel years younger and lighter!

When I cleaned out my office, which was a 2 year procrastination, I threw out 12 bags of papers and old memories that don't serve me anymore. I had old notes, company paraphernalia, old bank statements, receipts, you name it. But I also found papers that could resurrect a coaching business I was very active in a number of years ago. I was changing people's lives when I was doing that coaching. So I had something very important to think about; should I resurrect that business and change some more lives in that area? Should I put energy into that?

What actually happened was even better. I got the idea to start a coaching business in the niche I'm in now, helping entrepreneurs market their business online. I was surprised I hadn't thought of it before.

Then I realized I had blocked the idea from coming to me—because of my lack of peace of mind. Before my MDD I was feeling completely overwhelmed and stressed from having so many undone things swirling around in my mind all the time.

When I cleaned out my basement (another 3 year procrastination), it wasn't just my own stuff I sifted through, all the things I thought I loved and cared about. My children are both in their 20s, and they left their prized possessions with me when they moved out. I got to teach them about the MDD, and have them go through the same process of determining "What is important to me?", "What serves me and what can I let go of for good?" Teaching them that was very special to me. Doing an authentic MDD is unique and is deeper than a spring cleaning of your house. Going through the training is the only way to get the real understanding of what a MDD is and how it works in your life. How it can impact your thinking and your behavior going forward. And here's another reason to do your MDD now, rather than later. One of the things on my list was to go through all the boxes in my basement. Some of the boxes had been packed 3 years before and never unpacked in my new home.

I found all of our family pictures; I looked at pictures I hadn't seen in years, and since the pictures made my list of my most important possessions, it hit me really hard that I hadn't had them close to me, they'd been packed away. I had denied myself the happiness of having them around me, so my MMD has brought me ongoing joy.

I got so much pleasure going through all those pictures!
I found precious pictures I didn't remember ever seeing. I found pictures of my Mom playing cards with my daughter, and teaching my son to play solitaire. My Mom has been gone 6 years now, and these are memories I didn't even know I had.

I found the note my mother wrote to my son right before he started kindergarten.

Two other pictures I had never seen before, that touched my heart and gave me such joy—and new memories! My kids at 2 and 4 relaxing and watching Winnie the Pooh at my sister's house; Kate has her arm on Brian, and then on his head. Special moments of pure love.

I also found the rare pictures of me with my children when they were young (I was always the one taking the pictures—with a camera—so I'm in very few of them!)

Oh the things you'll find during your MDD!
I found the Venetian glass necklace my daughter brought back from Venice for me; I had been looking for this necklace for 8 years! I couldn't remember where I put it and I thought it was gone forever. I found it in a box I had gone through several times previously. That mystified me that I had never found it before. I think I was being much more thorough and clear because I was in the MDD mindset, and it paid off!

A MDD also gave me the opportunity to give things away too. In addition to the tons of clothes and household items I gave away, I was able to give special keepsakes away too.
One of my best helpers was my friend Bobbi's daughter Sydney, whom she adopted from Russia. I went to the Soviet Union when I was in high school, and brought back a set of Russian nesting dolls, so I gave them to her as a memento.

I also made a monumental decision during my MDD. I decided I was not going to take all my possessions to CA. I decided to take only what would fit in my car, and take only the things that were most important to me. So I hired a company that comes to your house and takes all your stuff. They sell what they can, donate what they can, and throw out the rest. It was a huge relief to come to this decision. I saved myself massive amounts of money, time and effort letting most of my stuff go.

Cleaning my office, the basement, and some closets gave me amazing feelings of renewal.

Laurie Conrod's Results

One of my biggest mistakes was actually putting off doing my MDD! I knew I was contributing a chapter to this book, and it was time to do a full-on MDD. But I didn't do it right away, and 10 days later I broke my leg while I was sailing in a race. I was in a wheelchair for 3 months, and by the time I was mobile enough to start my MDD, I could only do a couple hours at a time, I still couldn't walk. I couldn't carry boxes or carry things from one room to another. It took me weeks to do something that I could have finished in a few days, and I had to have help. So don't procrastinate your MDD!

My MDD activities helped me resolve and create closure on things: I rediscovered pictures and mementos that reminded me of relationships and memories that no longer serve me. Finding these things, musing over the memories, and then throwing the items away was a cleansing experience; I highly recommend it!

One of the best outcomes for me of a MDD, is the residual feelings I've had after my MDD. I am ahead of procrastination now. It's hard to explain it. But every time I encounter a decision of whether to keep or take care of something in my life, I take it much more seriously and give the decision the time it deserves in the present moment, instead of storing it and saving it for later, putting it off. Later may not come for a long time, depleting my mental energy needlessly. This state of mind is a feeling that is beyond feeling refreshed. It's a consistent state of clarity. It's a state of being that gives me a clean slate every day to grow and flourish. And I love giving each decision in my life, small and large, the time it deserves.

A MDD helps you follow your dreams and live a life you design, instead of a life lived by default. Eliminating all the undone things in your life allows clear thinking, superb ideas to come to you, and ah-ha moments at the just the right time. I think most people are running at about 50% capacity, and they can't figure out why. Do a MDD and see how your ability to be productive increases dramatically. I've had the best ideas to grow my business come to me since my MDD.

I think it would be great for business owners to give employees a day off to do a MDD. It would improve their productivity and quality of life. Maybe make it an optional program, where they watch the training on their own time, and then when they have their list, they get a Friday off to do the MDD (and have the weekend to do more if needed). Then on Monday, share with the office their experience, and their results.

Laurie Conrod's 6 Tips

#1- All tasks weighing on your mind are important. Put everything on your list. Little things can create huge clearing and breakthroughs.

#2- Hire help (nieces, nephews, kids in the neighborhood) so you can make decisions and tell people to move stuff around, sort things, run up and down stairs, etc. Be the supervisor and you'll get a lot more done! And/or get a friend and help each other do each other's MDD.

#3- Organize your list the night before and decide where you want to start. I found that starting at the top of the house, and working down, is the best. There's usually less to deal with in bedrooms than basements!

#4- Make all the phone calls (doctor appointments, handyman appointments etc.) early in the day, it gives a fast feeling of accomplishment.

#6- Put on your favorite music (really loud) and enjoy all your accomplishments! Check off the items on your list as you complete them!

About Laurie Conrod

 Laurie Conrod lives in Southern California with her German Shepherd, Sophie. She spent 25 years working in corporate America, and made the transition to entrepreneurship with a coaching business in 2006 when the life of commuting, being stuck in an office, and being told what to do all the time became unbearable. Then she discovered how to have a business online, instead of trading time for money, allowing even more freedom to grow as an entrepreneur. Now she helps other entrepreneurs grow their business online, or start a new one.

When she's not on her laptop, she loves to sail and race yachts, travel, explore California, and spend time with family and friends.

She's passionate about self-development: One of the greatest gifts of being human is the joy of growing spiritually, in leadership skills, entrepreneurially, and following our desires. She believes entrepreneurship is a vehicle to finding out who you really are, and what you're capable of.

She helps entrepreneurs grow their business through her coaching club, www.onlineentrepreneurclub.com.

"I believe we should all love what we do, and be prosperous doing it. The wealthier we are in all areas of our lives, the more we can give to the world."

You can contact Laurie at www.laurieconrod.com, or email her at laurie@laurieconrod.com.

Troy Scott

Ironically, as I type this introduction to Troy's chapter, he just texted me with a thrilling update that his online businesses are popping him $1500 checks over and over from a business he created. He is nailing the online process, enjoying more time and location freedom, and growing in his level of contribution to the world.

But, as you will discover in his chapter, he went "online" after a devastating business failure. Amidst the ruins of a collapsed dream, he discovered the "Million Dollar Day."

He took his MDD seriously. Very seriously. And it created a lifestyle audit that reset EVERYTHING. Like Jamie Waters' story in an early chapter, Troy and his wife fixed a myriad of "money leaks" in their financial life.

But even more than that, the MDD added a sense of calm and creative power back into their lives. Once the clutter was cleared (both financially, environmentally in their home and offices, and even relationally) the stage was set for a productive onslaught.

I'm grateful Troy invested the time to share the nitty-gritty details of his day. He has been a wind of encouragement to me, and I trust his story will inspire you as well. Enjoy!

Everyone remembers the technology success stories from the news. You know the general storyline idea, just build an app and sell it, right? Facebook spent $19 billion on (remember WhatsApp?) and now the co-founders, Jan Koum and Brian Acton, are both billionaires, sounds simple doesn't it? The results that make up the news story rarely ever report on the failures that lead up to those dramatic outcomes.

Living in Silicon Valley, I've seen it first hand how technology can explode someone's net worth. I've watched my friend's medical software company get acquired for hundreds of millions, another have success with a Google acquisition and I personally know a few Facebook millionaires who retired from that IPO a few years back.

The reality is that these types of success stories (sans major corporations) will only continue because the proliferation and subsequent adoption of new technology will never stop. Technology is making it possible for anyone to succeed.

From my view, I see the rise of the digital entrepreneur. A completely new world developing all around with significantly less publicized success stories happening everyday. In today's digital world, you can create your own success in a relatively short amount of time compared to the old "Business as Usual" world.

Today, success stories like creating your first online sale, or creating an online course to sell your knowledge into a market place are taking the place of the more common roads to financial success like buying stocks, or discovering how to leverage a real estate deal.

To me, these new success stories are just as exciting as the folks who are working to develop new technology or creating the next big app.

What's more, in today's technological environment, the barrier to creating your own business has been smashed to pieces. Today, there is no longer a barrier. Just log onto GoDaddy, buy a domain name, set up an offer and drive traffic. Sure, there is a little bit more to it than that, but broken down into the simplest of terms . . . that's kinda how it works.

Today's growing faction of digital nomads operate with a different mindset governed by a completely new set of belief systems. We're seeing teenage Youtube stars, making more than their parents and personal brands created out of thin air on Instagram or Snapchat.

We've entered the era of what I call "Thought Technology" where building networks of people who think and feel the same way as the entrepreneur driving the action. They coexist, they become a tribe . . . the size of your tribe is directly correlated by the amount of value you bring to the market. Developing your personal brand network across various platforms is the next frontier.

The killer app is figuring out how to leverage value and technology into the global marketplace.

Most people don't fail enough. Most people give up way too soon, or worse yet they settle.

Learn to embrace your journey and break on through to the other side . . . as our old friend Jim Morrison once suggested.

It may take a few "at bats" but when you take that swing . . . breathe it in . . . because you're no longer in the stands watching my friend . . . you're in the game! Where you should be.

Few talk about the massive failures that often time make up the steps to success.

This is one of those tales . . . where bad timing, massive failure and the Million Dollar Day changed everything.

Over Leveraged, Dumb Decisions and a Bad TV Deal

I remember the day like it was yesterday. I fell back into my seat and immediately placed both of my hands on my face . . . thinking to myself, OH MY GOD.

I couldn't believe it, another business and another total failure. Even though it was against my wife's wishes, I still bet the farm on it . . . and lost $50,000! It was all of our capital. The problem was, we were already living on credit cards and I just flushed all of our liquid finances down the drain.

Before learning about "The Million Dollar Day", (roughly a year prior) I was sitting motionless in my home office, slumped over in my chair . . . staring like a zombie at my computer screen. What was I going to do . . . I was lost, this was supposed to be our ticket out of this financial mess I created.

I was in complete shock. I had just concluded a phone call with my business partner where I learned we were not going to recover a dime of the $50k we each invested. $100,000 gone. Call me stupid (I was). Call me naïve (I was). Call it looking at the opportunity through rose-tinted glasses (yup that too). What this business idea did not have, looking back on it now, was a solid execution plan.

In fact, most of my failures share similar characteristics.
All of the investment money we spent up front for contractors, the entire production team, camera crew, the equipment rental fees, the sound engineer, and the big satellite switcher truck were great for everyone who got paid. For us however, it was a complete and total loss.

But, that's "business as usual" compared with internet marketing. High risk, zero returns (most of the time) vs. low risk and your success directly correlates to how hard you work.

Everyone got paid but us. Sure there was a few grand left, but after all the bills were paid, it was a big fat doughnut, except for the pain and psychological torment of having gone through it. I could have shorted the failure timeline considerably, eliminated any related hope I had associated with a positive outcome and achieved the exact same results by just taking the $50k and tossing it out the window.

You see, earlier that year, we had just wrapped up production shooting a made for TV MMA (mixed martial arts) event at the Orange County Convention Center in Los Angeles. We had solid phone calls, and industry insight, that all the content we had lined up to shoot and produce (more on that later), in addition to the MMA fight, that the networks we had pitched were interested. There are no contracts in retail sales for television (unless you have backdoor deals), you produce a product and then you sell it, THEN you get paid after it airs.

So we went out and shot our first event with the intention of selling it and getting this big production machine up and running.

We produced a network level television production, a similar type of set-up you would see the UFC (Ultimate Fighting Championship) or Showtime Sports shoot. In fact, we had 3 of the traveling UFC's cameramen that day. My Co-Founder worked at Digital CBS Los Angeles and took care of the entire production side of the business. My responsibility was curating content, branding and marketing. The plan was simple. Shoot the fight in a new cutting edge way that took advantage of SAP (Secondary Audio Programming) and simultaneously produce the event in both Spanish and English (which we did) 2-sets of announcers called it live back to the switcher truck. We just needed to package it up and sell it into both markets.

Everything worked great except for that last part, selling it.

All I have now is a few very expensive Sports Alive t-shirts and the equivalent of a few gold-plated hard drives with content I'll never sell. What my partner and I didn't know at the time was the massive consolidation taking place "upstairs" industry term, within the target networks we were talking to.

Literally overnight, everything changed for us and that's when things went from bad to worse. At the network level, new programming buys were extremely secretive or put on hold as industry news started to come out. Soon the stories about these changes went public, as the television production model started to radically shift. Actors like Rob Lowe were tweeting about how horrible it was that entire production teams were getting whacked in Hollywood.

What we didn't know (what you don't know is quite common with Business As Usual) were all of the internal challenges taking place behind closed doors at the networks.

Even though we spent a lot of time planning this out, it may have been the worst possible time to try and sell a product like this. Consolidation with technology, production outsourcing and the seismic industry shifts in how television content was now being curated, produced and consumed started to radically affect TV production. Very much the same way technology disruption has affected other industries like that of Uber or Airbnb.

Big TV Networks started buying other TV Networks as Comcast bought NBC Universal and created the NBC SPORTS NETWORK. Then FOX SPORTS went public with the news that they had purchased the rights to the SPEED Network and then later announced they planned on killing the SPEED brand to make way for FOX SPORTS 1 and 2 with the intentions of changing the format completely.

It didn't matter that we had contracts with other sporting events and promoters to shoot and produce for SPEED. Heck SPEED was re-airing two shows through Lucas Oil On The Edge that I had coordinated the production of, we even had all the relationships in place!

The SPEED Network was now dead, we were sitting on a show that no one wanted, and our futures play on SPEED just died. Our timing to pitch TV content could not have been worse. It was a complete disaster. It was official. It was game over for us.

The biggest challenge with this type of business model, besides having good compelling content, is that you have enormous upfront capital costs for production. This type of business requires that you build the product first, unless you package production into a "futures-type" of arrangement that lets you invest the proceeds into future productions and sell multiple shows. This exact model is why you see so many reality TV shows, appear and then disappear just as fast . . . massive losses, typically. Conversely . . . everyone knows about the "Housewives of Atlanta" or Beverly Hills or name a city . . . series. Same model, only that one worked.

As an entrepreneur, a certain amount of failure should be expected and honestly, it's a rite of passage of sorts. Think of it as the "universe" kicking you around a bit in order to see what you're made of.

The path to success is not easy and I've come to realize that failure is there to "toughen you up" and remind you of it. The universe rewards persistence, tenacity, and drive. One of my mentors calls it an "affliction," this entrepreneurship thing . . . he's right, it is.

The dream is what drives us and making your dreams become a reality is truly possible. I've been able to do it on a number of occasions and it's not always been business related.

Having a dream or vision for yourself is very important, it keeps you alive, at least that's my view. I don't want to be that guy that's surrounded by his grandchildren expounding regrets . . .

I wanted to tell fantastic stories.

This was business failure number 3 for me. Anyone who goes out and tries to make something happen will eventually realize that success is a process not an event.

Still in shock, after receiving the news, I asked myself . . . what was I going to do? This was a big deal, this was a major loss, and this decision, I would eventually learn, could put my family in bankruptcy. Leaning back in my chair, thoughts of panic began to swirl around in my head. I tried to put it out of my mind for at least the afternoon until my wife got home. Worst case I thought, I could go and get a job with one of my first investors, I told myself.

Typically, I deal with stress and overwhelm by diving into a project or completely losing myself in work activities, but this hit was different . . . I just wiped out all of our cash. To make matters worse, we weren't in the greatest place financially to begin with and we had been struggling for a while. I was now rethinking everything.

My wife, Cathy . . . thank god, is an entrepreneur too. Mainly on her success we weathered the storm. Fed up with being employed in the tech industry and the boom and bust startup cycle of Silicon Valley, she came home one day and made the decision to start her own business. She's awesome and within just a few months, she was able replace her income and create a successful pet sitting business in San Jose.

That was over 10 years ago.

Here's a little more background. Fast forward to August 2013 after bouncing around the internet looking for new business ideas, I quite literally stumbled on a webinar replay about an online business opportunity. In fact, it was a strange happenstance of Jonathan Bud, Mark Hoverson and Vincent Ortega Jr.—it may have been one of their first webinars together. Of course there was an offer . . .
After investigating further, what got my attention was that I could get all this incredible training that I was actually looking for at the time. The idea here was that it would help me create my next business.

The package of online courses being offered was right up my alley. Even more appealing to me, was that the whole package was being offered at a significant discount as part of a live event being promoted.

I was hungry and ready for a new venture. I had been looking to start in internet marketing business for the last year and I knew all of this training would help me create one. The promotion was actually the very first ILN event in Arizona. The purchase got me access to the event, but I couldn't go, I was completely broke. In fact, I had to actually borrow the money to buy the training . . . that's how bad things were.

Interesting, I didn't know it at the time but that stretch, the push I made to borrow the money . . . changed everything for me. That simple decision sent my entire entrepreneurship trajectory into the wonderful world of Internet Marketing and changed everything for me.

Packaged inside all of these other great online courses was this one little course called "The Million Dollar Day". That's funny, "cute title" I said, and passed it over to jump into something else I assumed was more important like the "Info Marketing Blueprint" and forgot about the MDD.

Now let's jump back to the day where I was slumped in my chair and staring at my computer monitor recovering from the news . . . trying to figure out how I was going to dig us out of this enormous mess. I had that feeling of being completely disorganized and aimless after the horrible news . . . I thought to myself, as many of us do from time to time . . . I need to clean this office up and get a fresh start. So that's what I began doing. I started going through the endless piles of paperwork and random sticky notes strewn about my desk area. Then for whatever reason, I glanced over and started looking at my whiteboard noticing all the old notes from months ago still on it.

What was interesting is what I had written at the top, "One Day You Will Make a Million Bucks"—a light bulb went off, "The Million Dollar Day" . . . that's it, I thought to myself, "I sure could use a million dollar day" right about now . . . not having a clue what the training was actually about. Right then and there, I decided to stop everything and do this Million Dollar Day Thing.

One thing you realize right out of the gate is that this training is not what you think it is.

As the process unfolds, you begin to understand that this is way more than just another training online training course . . . This is life coaching, this is about eliminating procrastination, this is about getting your life re-organized, this is about mending broken relationships, this is about eating right, this is about self-worth . . . this is about getting your business priorities corrected, it's about connecting with your spouse, a loved one . . . I could go on and on because it's that powerful.

The timing for me to hear what Mark Hoverson had to say could not have been better.

Do not underestimate how much of an impact this can have on you your life and your family. Live it out loud and breathe it in.

Troy Scott's Results

The first few sections of the MMD were very interesting and quite revealing. It allowed me to see and realize just how out of balance I was, not only with my entrepreneurship, but with my health, exercise, and eating habits.

One of the more interesting aspects of the MDD is how you work through the process of actually adding up and tabulating the amount "time baggage" we carry around . . . useless mental baggage, and a complete waste of your brain power.

From the Completed Health List section for example, my procrastination was starting to show. I was already up to 6 years worth of baggage I was carrying around. I had either been thinking about doing the item, or started doing something, and then never even finished it.
Going through the process, I started to realize just how out of balance my life had actually developed into. My health, spending quality time with my wife, and the disaster that I let our personal finances become.

Sadly, I had realized the consistency I had in wasting money. Now completely broke, I was being forced to reevaluate everything.

I realized the true gravity of it all when we completed the Household List Section of the MDD. Broke and in need of tightening our belt, Cathy and I went to work on seeing what we could cut.

Admittedly, it was a little embarrassing as to how sloppy I was running our finances. In fact, I wasn't . . . Cathy was handling everything . . . it was her burden and I had not realized what I had put her through with all this risk-taking entrepreneurship I'd been involved with. Because of the MDD, I took the time and apologized to her and then we went to work.

Working through the Household List Section of the MDD is when it all started coming together for us. One of the items on our list was how often we had been talking about cleaning out our storage space. We had rented a massive storage space and just filled it to the top with crap. Stuff we just held onto, stuff we just did not need, stuff that was mental baggage.

The MDD helped us empty it.

Literally, for the better part of 5 years, we were living the lottery mentality. Both of us were doing really well financially. We acquired a second home, vacationed regularly and I bought lots of toys, dirtbikes, a tricked out 4x4 a camping trailer, and did lots of traveling and dirtbike racing.

Cathy's business was performing extremely well and things were going great for both of us. Then, as the pendulum tends to do, things began to slowly swing the other way. Market shifts, new technology trends, and a series of business failures began to catch up to us.

I kept telling Cathy that this next deal is gonna hit! We would finally be able to catch up and get this whole financial mess cleaned up. You know the old, "don't worry honey, everything will be fine," you know, those empty promises that some of us tell our spouses . . . because in reality, as partners, we're actually terrified of how we're actually going to pull it off . . . right?

What was really going on was that we were avoiding things, just prolonging the inevitable crash, getting by on credit cards and keeping up with a lifestyle that was in need of a change.

Here's a tip, get yourself in a position to lose it all, along with a boatload of cash and put your back up against the wall . . . it's a great way to usher in a major correction.

As I mentioned earlier, as an entrepreneur, the universe is always waiting to kick you around a little . . . to toughen you up, and see if you have what it takes to keep going.

I had created a big mess and it was time to start cleaning it up. The MDD gave us the framework to get started.

We started doing the math on everything . . . the extra stress, the bleeding of wasted dollars from a non-existent health club memberships to all the extra guilt and crap you carry around when you have money problems. You need to flush it all, this MDD thing can help.

For us the bigger picture was that the MDD process forced a complete financial audit of our household and business expenses, something that both Cathy and I had been avoiding for a long time. Because of the MDD, we found clarity. Life after the MDD is completely different then those desperate times from before. Today, my wife's business continues to grow and I help other entrepreneurs leverage technology to grow sales.

Troy Scott's 5 Tips

#1- Set an appointment with you and your spouse if you're married.

#2- If you're married, make this a special all weekend project. Start the process Friday night and watch the entire video and take notes. Wake up Saturday and watch it again then get to work. Sunday continue to take action! It will add another layer of connectivity to your marriage.

#3- Expect to feel a little overwhelmed. In fact, the more overwhelmed you feel about creating this list, the more you will get out of the experience.

#4- Do not underestimate how much of an impact this can have on you personally, your business and your family.

#5- Make sure you go through this training at least 3 times.

About Troy Scott

Entrepreneur | Digital Marketer | Internet Marketing Strategist

I help business owners set up proven on-line systems that grow their businesses faster and easier. Over the last 5 years I've combined content marketing strategies with automated systems to achieve over $50mm in sales.

Website: TroyScottGroup.com
Facebook: https://www.facebook.com/TSJVMG
LinkedIn: https://www.linkedin.com/in/troyscottjvmg
Instagram: https://www.instagram.com/troy_s_scott
Snapchat: Troy_jvmg

Victor Dedaj

Victor is a classic born and bred New Yorker. He has a financial mind. This chapter focuses on the financial benefits that were brought into his life upon engaging in the MDD. Here are my big two takeaways from his chapter:

#1- As you will read, he had a burdensome $9500 tax bill from the IRS. Admittedly, avoiding that fine is pretty natural because opening up conversations with the IRS is about as fun as eating worms inside a dark labyrinth filled with snakes and spiders. But the MDD gave him the courage and excuse to address the problem.

The result? Instead of paying the $9500, the IRS ended up sending him $400. That's a nearly $10,000 swing because he watched a 90-min video called the Million Dollar Day. Not bad.

#2- Victor also shares how he uncovered "forgotten" money from other accounts. Victor embraced the MDD so strongly, that it reoriented his relationship with money. The hustle-bustle of modern life has a tendency to blur our priorities. But the strength of Victor's story, is that he took the clarity of the MDD and got a new vision on how to earn, keep, and defend his money with courage and certainty. It's a romantic story of math.

Doing the Million Dollar Day changed my life. I have eliminated procrastination from my life, don't waste unnecessary time, and I received almost $6,000 since finishing the Million Dollar Day. I recently received $1,900 from a Health Savings account that terminated four years ago. I also got $4,000 from a $500 investment I made a few months ago.

I had heard about the Million Dollar Day from some of my Facebook friends. They told me it changed their lives and made them more productive and efficient in their lives, as well as in their businesses. I knew that I could do more with my life than I had been doing. I had the talent, but was not fully utilizing it. I realized it must be something I was either doing wrong, or something right I was not doing. Hence, I opted to try the Million Dollar Day.

Before the Million Dollar Day, I used to procrastinate a lot. I wanted to do and accomplish many things, but was waiting for the perfect situation to arrive before I would try new things. The perfect time never arrived. I did not realize that I had to take action first, and then things would take care of themselves and get done.

There were a lot of things I wanted to do. I did not realize that the clutter I had in my rooms symbolized the clutter I had in my life. Even when I worked in the corporate world, my desk was often messy. There were papers all over my cubicle. I noticed that most of the upper level management always had neat desks with all the papers placed away in folders or in their drawers. I used to wonder how is it no matter how busy the upper management got, their desks were always neat when they left to go home, and my desk was not. The executives made sure they found time to put away all the papers and to keep their desk neat. They were always in control, and did not feel powerless.

I also looked at what the procrastination did in my house and the tasks I performed at home. The unfinished stuff felt a like huge psychological burden on me. It prevented me from performing other tasks that I wanted to do. I would look at the piles of paper and piles of clothes in my room, and I would at times feel powerless to do the things I knew I needed to do. I just did not know what to do first because I felt paralyzed.

I would see some shirts and pants on my swivel chairs, and I knew I had to put them away, yet I felt I needed them there to be ready in case I wanted to wear them. I had papers such as old year end job reviews from 10 years ago, books from college, and credit card and bank statements from 10 years ago that I was never going to use or look at. I knew I needed to get rid of them, yet held on to them. When I got rid of the papers and the rest of the clutter, I felt freer. It felt like a huge burden was lifted off of me. Doing the Million Dollar Day got rid of the clutter in my life, and I am now able to focus and finish tasks in a timely manner. I prioritize tasks, and focus on the most important ones first. As I finish each task, I feel a sense of accomplishment. My mind feels freer, and I feel that I am more creative with my thinking, and I am attracting newer and better things. My rooms are clean, and I don't have clutter all around. It's easier to me to find things, and I rarely lose things.

Over a couple of years ago I was sent a notice by the Internal Revenue Service claiming that because of capital gains they alleged I received in 2009, I owed them about $9,500 in back taxes, interest, and penalties.

I knew that the figure from Internal Revenue Service was wrong, because I knew I suffered losses from transactions done by me through a financial services company. The financial services company for some reason provided a zero cost basis for my buys of index funds, and the IRS used that as a basis for charging me the $9,500 for the sells I later made. That was because with a zero cost basis, no matter how little I sold the index fund at, I would have a gain. If the financial services company had put in the actual cost basis for the index funds, the Internal Revenue Service would have seen losses for these index funds.

Normally I would have procrastinated in doing something, and when the deadline approached, I would have paid the fee just to get rid of the headache.

However, I decided to take action and opted to take the Internal Revenue Service to court. The Internal Revenue Service wrote me back asking me if I wanted to settle out of court. I looked at the history of the transactions on the financial services company's web site, and spoke to a person at the Internal Revenue Service. She was initially reluctant to look at the transactions, but then later changed her mind. The IRS woman agreed to do her own calculations, and after doing her calculations, she calculated that I was owed around $400 by the IRS. So instead of paying $9,500, I got back over $400, a difference of almost $10,000! Not procrastinating saved me $10,000.

Victor Dedaj's Results

Some of the good things that have happened as a result of getting rid of all this procrastination:

I don't worry about costs anymore in terms of educating myself, because the costs of not learning is more expensive than the cost of learning. In my previous online companies, I never wanted to pay for company events because it cost too much money. Now I go to all company events because I realize the value of going to those events.

I often used to buy stuff online and not take the time to see if there were any discounts or free shipping coupons available for those products. Now before I buy anything online, I go to see if there are coupon or discount codes. I would say by doing that I have saved about $300 this year. Why not look for money that is entitled to me? I am deserving of the savings.

I just got $4,000 this week for putting in $500 in a company three months ago, a return of 800%.

My Health Saving Account closed 4 years ago. I forgot about it. Soon after finishing the Million Dollar Day, the HSA company sent me a letter telling me I still had about $1,900 in it.

One major result of doing the Million Dollar Day and no longer procrastinating is that my mind is not weighed down by undone things that have been hanging around for years. A grand total of 20 years of procrastination has been eliminated from the actions below.

From the $1,900 I got for the Health Savings account and the $4,000 I got for the $500 investment, I have received $5,900 soon after finishing the Million Dollar Day.

What I have learned is that the first step is just to get the process started. The beginning of any journey begins with the first step. If you want the things around you to change, you have to change. I used to carry the past with me. Now I use the past to learn from, and live in the present, while planning for the future.

Even if it is something that will only take a minute, I take care of a task immediately so it does not linger in my mind as something that will eventually have to get done.

Victor Dedaj's 4 Tips

#1- Clean up the clutter in your house and at your work space, and you'll clean up the clutter in your life. You'll be amazed at how efficient and productive you become.

#2- Prepare a list of things to do each day. Prioritize your list and do the important ones first, and feel a sense of accomplishment.

#3- Expect to feel overwhelmed and a sense of dread.

#4- Get up early to get ready for the day.

About Victor Dedaj

Victor Dedaj is a Traveling FreedomPreneur and Foodpreneur. He is a lifelong New Yorker who spent many years working in the corporate world, before transitioning to the online marketing world, which he now absolutely loves.

Victor enjoys the freedom, flexibility and lifestyle he now has as an internet entrepreneur, as well as living the lap top lifestyle, and being able to work from any place in the world.

As a foodpreneur, Victor loves sampling all the various ethnic cuisines throughout the world. His view is "Food determines mood."

Victor Dedaj can be contacted in the following ways:
Email: victor_p_dedaj@yahoo.com
Facebook: https://www.facebook.com/victor.dedaj.3
Twitter: @victordedaj
Instagram: at @victordedaj
Pinterest: http://pinterest.com/victordedaj3

Victor Dedaj's web site is http://victordedaj.biz

6 More Products And Experiences
From The Hoverson Brand

THE GREAT
LEMONADE CRUSADE

A few years ago, the kids and I stopped by a Lemonade Stand a kid was doing. The little cup of lemonade was warm. It had dust in it. The kid put her fingers all over the rims of the cups before she gave them to us. The kid didn't smile at us. Didn't say thanks. Nothing. And the lemonade was watered-down and pretty gross.

So I asked the kids, "Do you think that lemonade stand was for us? Or was it just for her to make money?" The all said, "Well, it wasn't for us."

A week later, I stopped at another stand. It was equally horrible. So, despite the fact that I was launching two companies at that time, and working about 15 hour days, I spent several hours that day creating a real-life "game" for kids to play.

They scored points for building a "5-Star Lemonade Stand." And we gave away new iPads, Amazon Kindles, new Nikes, Cash, all sorts of stuff to inspire "personal best" efforts.

And to my surprise, the game took off! It's entirely free to play, and kids & parents rave about the whole experience. We are ALWAYS looking for more leaders and sponsors.

My vision is to have as much excitement around youth entrepreneurship as there is around youth sports. The movement is moving, check it out here:

www.lemonadecrusade.com

When I was in 8th grade, my pastor challenged me to read one chapter of Proverbs per day from the Bible. There are 31 chapters, and 31 days per month. I took up the challenge, and have now read the book literally thousands of times.

But instead of just "reading" the verses, I began to "visualize" and "feel" each verse manifesting in my life 100%. I also began to scribble notes next to each verse, cataloguing whether they were about "speech", "learning", "humility", "money", etc.

Years ticked by, and wasn't until I started my business that I realized that so many of those verses were about money and business. So, although we qualified for welfare at the time, I began to reimagine each business verse manifesting in my enterprises.

And, although I won't blame you for not believing me, I went from qualifying for welfare to earning over $5 Million is just a few years.

But there began a gnawing concern in the back of my mind. I thought, "What if I died early, and my kids didn't know about how to apply Solomon's wisdom into their lives? What if they grew up thinking all this success was just some sort of fluke?"

So I an entire brand around Solomon's wisdom. And not only has it earned me millions, the reports of how the course has absolutely revolutionized people's financial lives is amazing. We have a free sample and action guide to for you to check out here:

www.discoversolomon.com

SOLOMON LIFE

My Solomon obsession took hold after "Solomon CEO" was a commercial success. People's businesses began to lift as their minds and hearts were set free to pursue their entrepreneurial gifts without apology or guilt. I began to see myself sort of like a museum curator, who was collecting and displaying (and restoring) the ancient wisdom of Solomon back into the main streets of the modern marketplace.

However, I had a perplexing reality in my life. I realized that while I had mastery over the "creation" of wealth, I was clueless over the "preservation and multiplication" of wealth. I had tried the stock market. But I started making money in 2007, and in 2008, the market dove about 38%. So I did not trust the idea that I would pack away money into the market, only to have the possibility of it taking a nose-dive during my retirement years.

On top of that, almost every single week, I had clients and colleagues asking me where I was putting my money for retirement. I had no answers I was comfortable or confident sharing. Eventually, when it dawned on me that I was a big spender on virtually every area of my life EXCEPT my future, I went on a two-year hunt to find the safest and best retirement vehicle to "leave an inheritance to my children's children" (Proverbs 13:22).

So after I discovered it and began using it, I learned that about 85% of Fortune 500 Executives also use it too. It is one of the most common money-retaining strategies the 1% have used for over 100 years (including Walt Disney, Ray Croc of McDonald's and many other titans). So, as is my common practice when I love something, I start a company around it. It's called "Solomon LIFE" and is designed to restore generational prosperity back into the American families.

We made you a special, and short, video to explain it to you here:

www.mysolomonlife.com

LIMITL≡SS

Long story short, I randomly met a college kid in a cigar bar one day. He wanted to be an entrepreneur. We ended up visiting for an hour or so. The next day, he asked if I'd meet with a couple of his friends over a cigar and share a bit more, so I did.

Fast forward a few months, and we had 30 or so college kids packed into a cigar bar to ask me questions about wealth and business.

Then, they started inviting their friends from other states to show up and hear what I had to say about life and business. So eventually, to let the ideas spread to a wider audience, we launched something we called "LIMITLESS".

It now attracts some of the world's best and brightest young guys. It's by "interview-only", and the guys do quarterly "adventure master-minds" all over America like surfing, skiing, mountain-climbing and biking, and more.

If you know of a sharp, ambitious, positive, socially-confident young entrepreneur or executive-minded guy between the ages of 18-30 years old. Feel free to share with him this website to take a peek at the LIM-ITLESS culture, and if he so desires, he may request an interview below the video at this website:

www.playlimitless.com

INVISIBLE EMPIRE

If you have a business, or WANT to have a business go online, our team has created a step-by-step (click-by-click) experience on how to build a digital empire online EXACTLY as I have. It's arguably the most-complete and transparent course ever produced in the online space. We have entrepreneurs from all over the world experience their online breakthrough by going through our INVISBLE EMPIRE experience. We created a video to explain the details to you here:

www.yourinvisibleempire.com

**YOUR LIFESTYLE
PASSPORT**

I grew up a poor kid in land-locked North Dakota. I'd watch TV shows like "Crocodile Dundee", and I'd want to go to Australia. I'd watch "Miami Vice" and dream of spending time in Florida. I'd watch Magic Johnson play for the Lakers, and those old "Disney" specials on Sunday night that would have commercials for Disneyland. All of it enchanted me. I wanted to see the world. I wanted to travel. I wanted to explore. I wanted adventure.

So when the entrepreneurial bug seized me completely at age 27, I knew I needed a product to sell. And after hunting around the internet, I found a travel club that had an "affiliate program." I figured I should "own" the product if I was going to sell it. So I bought into the club. And immediately I took my first trip to Hawaii. I paid $298 for a two-bedroom condo right on the ocean.

I was hooked on the value of this club instantly. And in the first year as an affiliate, I personally sold about a million dollars of the product. After a few years, the owner of the company asked me if I ever thought of buying the company from him. I was shocked. I said, "Not really."

So we met in Scottsdale, Arizona. And we came to the table with the exact same purchase price in our minds. And with a bit of terror, I drained every single dollar I had to purchase the company. At the time of this writing, we have over 77,000 members from all over the world. It's one of the greatest purchases I've ever made for my family.

My entire "Adventurepreneur" brand was launched around my exploits while using this club. Whether Shanny and I are scouting whales off the coast of Hawaii. Or the kids and I are carving down mountains in Colorado, it's the club (with up to 90% off Expedia's pricing) that has made it all happen.

If you have a wanderlust bug like I do, or you are interested in earning a sweet commission as an affiliate of the club, check out the product here:

www.mylifestylepassport.com

Printed in Great Britain
by Amazon

10084518R00061